Praise for *Brooklyn by Name*:

"Taking off from neighborhood names, this page-turner of a book tells of the successive waves of settlers and immigrant arrivals who have given Brooklyn its distinctive flavor. Here are the men and women whose fantasies, foibles, and otherwise-fleeting fame find permanency in the pavements, parks and place-names of the borough that almost wasn't part of New York. This book will fascinate even the most provincial of non-Brooklynites. You don't have to live there to love this one."

— **Andrew Alpern, coauthor of** *New York's Architectural Holdouts*

"This wonderfully informative compendium of street and place names connects the past to today by recalling the diverse cast of characters who gave their names to Brooklyn. Jump into your walking shoes, bring along this marvelous book, and get ready to explore Brooklyn's streets!"

— **Judith Stonehill,**
coauthor of *Brooklyn: A Journey through the City of Dreams*

"In 1935 Thomas Wolfe published a short story in The New Yorker entitled 'Only the Dead Know Brooklyn,' which began with a man declaring 'Dere's no guy livin' dat knows Brooklyn t'roo an' t'roo, because it'd take a guy a lifetime just to find his way aroun' duh f—— town.' This is a sentiment that still applies even to this day when the Brooklynese accent that Wolfe sought to convey is as rare as a charlotte russe. But compared to rectilinear Manhattan, Brooklyn still remains a challenging hodge podge, a quagmire, a macedoine. Leonard Benardo and Jennifer Weiss have wisely stopped short of trying to demystify the place 't'roo and t'roo.' Instead they set themselves the relatively more modest but attainable goal of tracking down the origins of the borough's street names and in this they have done just fine, laudably filling many gaps in knowledge."

— **Michael T. Kaufman,**
former "About New York" columnist for the *New York Times*

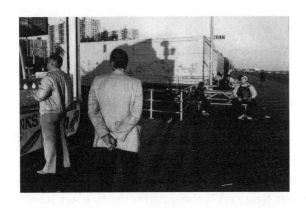

Brooklyn by Name

How the Neighborhoods, Streets, Parks,
Bridges, and More Got Their Names

Leonard Benardo and Jennifer Weiss

 New York University Press New York and London

ABOUT THE FRONT COVER:
TOP: Coney Island 1983, Photo by Anders Goldfarb
CENTER: Shore Parkway, 1970s, Photo by Jerry Tobias
BOTTOM LEFT: Brooklyn Bridge, Courtesy of Tom Ginocchio Collection, Brooklyn
RIGHT: Fulton Street, August 12, 1915, Courtesy of New York Transit Museum

ABOUT THE BACK COVER:
BOTTOM RIGHT: Tennis Court, Postcard (unknown origin), in authors' possession
BOTTOM LEFT: Brooklyn Academy of Music, 1923, Postcard (unknown origin), in authors' possession

NEW YORK UNIVERSITY PRESS
New York and London
www.nyupress.org

Library of Congress Cataloging-in-Publication Data
Benardo, Leonard.
Brooklyn by name : how the neighborhoods, streets, parks, bridges, and more got their names / Leonard Benardo and Jennifer Weiss.
p. cm.
Includes bibliographical references and index.
ISBN–13: 978–0–8147–9945–1 (cloth : alk. paper)
ISBN–10: 0–8147–9945–0 (cloth : alk. paper)
ISBN–13: 978–0–8147–9946–8 (pbk. : alk. paper)
ISBN–10: 0–8147–9946–9 (pbk. : alk. paper)
1. Brooklyn (New York, N.Y.)—History.   2. New York (N.Y.)—History.
3. Names, Geographical—New York (State)—New York—History.
I. Weiss, Jennifer.   II. Title.
F129.B7B48   2006
974.7'23—dc22   2005037706

New York University Press books are printed on acid-free paper,
and their binding materials are chosen for strength and durability.

Manufactured in the United States of America

c 10 9 8 7 6 5 4 3 2 1
p 10 9 8 7 6 5 4

For Felix,
who traversed this great borough with us—
on foot, subway, bus, and stroller.

Contents

List of Maps

Acknowledgments

In the course of writing this book, we were extremely fortunate to be supported by a large number of people. John Manbeck, Eric Wakin, Justin Burke, Andrew Alpern, and Gary Madavoy offered invaluable insights and prevented us from costly errors. Neighborhood historians Victoria Hofmo, Lee Rosenzweig, Ira Kluger, and Brian Merlis enlightened us with their local expertise. Ron Schweiger and Judith Stonehill provided necessary and well-timed encouragement. We offer special thanks to David Elligers for his extraordinarily generous contributions and rigorous critique of the myths of New Utrecht. Thanks to Amy Peck from the Prospect Park Alliance for her time and editorial input. And for anyone curious about New York City's palimpsest, we find Kevin Walsh's unparalleled on-line resource Forgotten NY to be required reading.

We cannot overstate our thanks to the incredible group at the Brooklyn Public Library, Brooklyn Collection, that assisted us with the bulk of our research: Judith Walsh, Joy Holland, Elizabeth Harvey, Susan Aprill, and June Koffi. Working with such a dedicated, passionate, and knowledgeable team, we quickly made the Brooklyn Collection our second home. We were also fortunate that the Brooklyn Historical Society reopened its library in time for us to avail ourselves of its rich holdings.

We are grateful to the individuals who helped in gathering photographs to illustrate our book, Erik Huber, John Hyslop, and Judith Todman at the Queens Public Library, Long Island Division, and Carey Stumm at the archives of the New York Transit Museum. We also offer our appreciation to Michael Vachon, who provided us with John Vachon's photographs of John Lindsay, and to Tom Ginocchio for his historic photos of the Brooklyn Bridge.

Writing this book also gave us the opportunity to become acquainted with some highly talented photographers whose work we feature and whose friendship we now enjoy—in particular, Lucille Fornasieri Gold and Anders Goldfarb, as well as our cartographer and Old Stone House aficionado Peter Joseph. Thanks also to Peter Fabry for taking the time to discuss his father's Brooklyn murals.

A very special thanks to our editor, Ilene Kalish of NYU Press, for her direction and encouragement, to Salwa Jabado for her care and assistance and, not least, to Despina Papazoglou Gimbel and Charles Hames, for their meticulous attention to the book's layout and design. To our families who offered unstinting support, and friends, who took an active interest and served as a sounding board while we slogged away, we say thank you. Last, we would like to acknowledge Henry Moscow, whose book on Manhattan was the chief inspiration for our own.

Brooklyn by Name

Introduction

> With each homey crash-crash crash-crash of the wheels against the
> rails, there would steal up at me along the bounding slopes of the
> awnings the nearness of all those streets in middle Brooklyn named
> after generals of the Revolutionary War.
> —Alfred Kazin, *A Walker in the City* (1951)

Brooklyn's identity has developed out of the shared associations of its landmark names. Coney Island, Prospect Park, Fulton Street, and Ebbets Field
are widely recognized and need little formal introduction. As totems of the
borough's culture and history, they continue to stir the popular imagination.

The streets and places of Brooklyn are the real arteries of the thriving
metropolis, and the sources of their names reveal the borough's and the nation's rich and textured past. Yet outside of the easily discernible, the origin
of many of Kings County's street and place-names remains obscure and
their derivations known only by the few. As Brooklyn historian Ralph Foster Weld dryly observed over a half century ago, "These names are repeated
glibly in many accents—unconscious tribute which the heedless present
pays to Brooklyn's past."

Understanding the history of names—the field of toponomy—opens a
unique window onto the past and offers an avenue to celebrate those left to
posterity. It is also a means of painting, in Terrence Ranger's evocative
phrasing, a more usable historical canvas. Brooklyn's street and place-
names run the gamut, representing signers of the Declaration of Independence, baseball greats, philosophers, poets, diplomats, saints—not to
mention the Revolutionary War generals whom Alfred Kazin makes reference to in his classic Brooklyn childhood memoir. A *tour d'horizon* of
Brooklyn names is, at once, an amble through the borough's history.

Mapping the Names

Brooklyn, whose earliest inhabitants comprised different groups of Native
Americans, is geographically situated in Western Long Island. But unlike
other parts of Long Island, which display a veritable bounty of Indian
names from Massapequa to Ronkonkoma, Brooklyn has only a handful.
Canarsie and Gowanus exist, to be sure, but Kings County's European
settlers ultimately adopted far fewer Native American names than other
parts of the metropolitan area.

Street names designating Dutch landowners are among the earliest acknowl-edged in Brooklyn. Remembered here are Brooklyn's noteworthy first families —the Lotts, Remsens, and Bergens—some with multiple namings scattered across the borough (being six towns originally, Brooklyn is rife with repetition). All told, landowners and developers are represented in the greatest number.

The British takeover inevitably led to linguistic corruption as, for exam-ple, *Boswijck* turned into "Bushwick" and *V'Lacke Bos* became "Flatbush." Anglicization also introduced names of English and royalist heritage—for example, Stirling, York, and not least, Kings County. In addition, Dutch fam-ilies were forced to take on surnames, rather than continue the custom of us-ing one's place of origin or patronymic. (Pieter Claeson [son of Claes], to take one example, adopted the name Wyckoff to satisfy the new sovereigns.)

Similar to the aftermath of other successful revolutions, following the Revolutionary War some streets were stripped of names associated with the *ancien régime* (though others, say for Tory sympathizer Joris Rapelye, sneaked through). In their stead were streets dedicated to the heroes of the conflict, from generals to infantrymen. International partisans who helped the revolution succeed were also honored with streets, including Lafayette (French), De Kalb (German), and Kosciuszko (Polish).

Street and place-names of this period additionally reflect the slavehold-ing culture once manifest throughout Kings County. The "peculiar institu-tion" had ignominious roots in Brooklyn and continued until its final abolition in 1827. At least seventy street names can be conclusively attrib-uted to the area's slaveholders.

The nineteenth century brought a new bevy of names associated with the War of 1812 and the Union Army in the Civil War, not to mention the first of several historical appeals to the founding fathers. Many signers of the Declaration of Independence were recognized with streets in Williams-burg, and accomplished military leaders—naval commanders being a par-ticular favorite—criss-crossed the streets of Bedford-Stuyvesant.

At the nineteenth century's end, place-names sought not only to honor a virtuous national past but also to reflect a sensibility that resonated with an increasing number of Brooklyn's elite. With the British no longer a mortal enemy and Victorian aesthetics of significant bourgeois appeal, English names were reintroduced as Brooklyn experienced a distinct wave of An-glophilia. Neighborhoods like Prospect Park South, Ditmas Park, Fort Greene, Manhattan Beach, and Kensington were the beneficiaries of as-sorted Anglo-rich street names like Cumberland, Argyle, Albemarle, Cam-bridge, and Oxford. What H. L. Mencken once mocked as Anglomania was a growth industry and included the precious substitution of "courts," "places," and "drives" for "streets."

Brooklyn was no stranger to the idiosyncrasies of American nationalism, witnessed by the several Prussian-sounding streets renamed during and following World War I. As the country swapped "frankfurter" for "hot dog" and "sauerkraut" for "liberty cabbage," so too did East New York's Vienna Avenue become Lorraine Avenue.

The post–World War II era has seen few changes in Brooklyn's names, apart from those lost to the wrecking ball—whether from the construction of the Brooklyn-Queens Expressway or the Belt Parkway. What has emerged instead is the secondary naming of streets for veterans, public servants, and other community leaders. Additionally, scores of streets have received subsidiary namings for those killed on September 11, 2001. These naming decisions are made by the New York City Council, as they once were by the Board of Aldermen.

A Very Short Sketch of the History of Brooklyn

The first recorded people to settle in Brooklyn were the Canarsee, an Algonquin-speaking tribe of the Delaware (Leni Lenape) Indians. With the arrival of the Dutch West India Company in 1625, ensuing violence, trade, appropriation of land, and war ultimately led to the Canarsee's flight and disappearance.

Over several decades, the Dutch West India Company offered charters to those ready to establish a permanent presence. The first went to settling Breukelen (Brooklyn) in 1646, predating by a decade New Amsterdam itself; then Nieuw Amersfoort (Flatlands) in 1647; Midwout (Flatbush) in 1652; Nieuw Utrecht (New Utrecht) in 1657; and finally, with Peter Stuyvesant's active participation, Boswijck (Bushwick) in 1661. Gravesend was the only one of the six original towns that was settled not by the Dutch but by the English—notably, by Lady Deborah Moody, who received a patent in 1645. For over two hundred years, Brooklyn was just one (albeit the largest) of the area's six towns.

The Dutch period was followed, beginning in 1664, with an English presence that lasted until the end of the War of Independence. Kings County—for King Charles II of England—was formally established in 1683 to be one of New York's ten counties, and its central institutions were located in Flatbush, the county's geographic center.

Despite the range of settlements, the overall population of Kings County by the time of the American Revolution was still a modest 3,500. The war itself traces its origins to Brooklyn, as the very first battles in New York took place around today's Prospect Park and Gowanus areas. Like New York, all of Kings County was occupied during the war years, and the some 11,500 revolutionary captives who perished in squalid prisoner ships at Wallabout Bay are the starkest historical reminder of the war's brutality.

Slavery is undoubtedly the greatest blight on Brooklyn's colonial and early American history. Arriving first with the Dutch, by 1800 it is estimated that of the five thousand persons living in Kings County, nearly one-third were slaves, a number proportionally greater than anywhere else north of the Mason-Dixon line. Indeed, various pockets of Brooklyn remained ambivalent on the issue. The city's flagship publication, the *Brooklyn Daily Eagle*, in fact removed its brilliant young editor, Walt Whitman, principally because of his quasi-abolitionist views.

It has been written that the nineteenth century in Brooklyn truly began with the *Nassau* ferry's maiden steam voyage across the East River. Several centuries of rowboat and other engineless travel were thrown to the wind in 1814 with Robert Fulton's creation, which proved to have profound economic consequences for the city.

At a rate often surpassing New York City itself, Brooklyn was rapidly developing into a thriving metropolis via its waterfront, industrial diversity, and influx of newcomers, and capped by the construction of the fabled Brooklyn Bridge. With its annexation of Williamsburg and Bushwick in 1855, Brooklyn became overnight the third most populous city in the United States. Over the next four decades Brooklyn progressively swallowed all its neighboring towns and villages so that by the century's end, it became coterminous with Kings County. Yet Brooklyn's empire building was short-lived: by the narrowest of margins, Brooklynites voted 64,744 to 64,467 in favor of consolidation with New York, and in 1898 Brooklyn the city became Brooklyn the borough.

In popular memory at least, the first half of the twentieth century is bound up with two central reference points: Coney Island as pleasure palace, working-class entertainment, and surreal fantasy; and the Brooklyn Dodgers, a signifier for the aspirations and dashed hopes of Brooklyn's own.

The Dodgers' heartrending departure for Los Angeles in 1957 signaled a transitional moment in Brooklyn's history. Alongside the construction of the Verrazano-Narrows Bridge and the attendant flight to the suburbs, the borough soon became engulfed in controversial issues of the day relating to race, immigration, education, and housing. With substantial demographic transformation, Brooklyn's population took on a changed profile and cast, and by the century's end it had become one of America's truly polyethnic places.

Outline of the Book and Caveats to the Reader

Our book is not an exhaustive study. As Thomas Wolfe famously put it, "It would take a lifetime to know Brooklyn. And even then, you wouldn't know it all." Brooklyn has over eighteen hundred streets, numbered and named (besting Manhattan severalfold), and hundreds of additional place-names including myriad bridges, parks, schools, and places of worship. We take Wolfe to heart and select herein a representative cross-section of the historically significant and culturally curious.

In the course of our research some name origins fell out of reach—even to neighborhood historians—and will hopefully be dredged up by future excavators. Others were self-explanatory—say, Parkside Avenue or President Street. Still others, like the numbered streets, didn't merit elucidation. Additionally, we have avoided by and large secondary street namings, focusing instead, with a handful of exceptions, on the street's primary name. In the end we have chosen roughly six hundred names that we hope will absorb and edify the reader. Nonetheless, we expect that our project will encourage others to fill in the blanks.

We faced a quandary in determining in which chapter to place a street that runs through multiple neighborhoods. Case in point: Bedford Avenue traverses Greenpoint in the north, through Bedford-Stuyvesant, all the way to Sheepshead Bay. Where possible, we have tried to select the area with which the street is most distinctly associated. Nonetheless, the index will be of use in identifying the street in question. Lastly, we have made every effort to hunt down the birth and death dates of individuals mentioned in the entries; in those cases where we were unsuccessful we hope that the details of the entry will provide a sufficient timeline.

Beginning with Brooklyn

One can find a wealth of permutations of Brooklyn's Dutch-era name—*Breukelen, Breuckelen, Breukelein, Bruijkleen, Broucklyn, Brucklyn*—on maps, historical records, and land deeds, though the received wisdom today has pretty much settled on Breukelen. Most scholars also agree that the name originates with the town in Utrecht, the Netherlands, from which the first Dutch settlers likely arrived. Following the English conquest, the name was anglicized to Brookland and, at some later point in the eighteenth century, corrupted to its present form. A common misconception that should be put to rest is that Brooklyn is Dutch for "broken land." The Dutch term *gebroken landt* (broken land) is actually the translation of the Algonquin name for Long Island and should not be confused with the origin of Brooklyn.

Before Brooklyn's 1898 incorporation into New York, debate ensued about the new borough's name; though never really in doubt, there were voices who sought to change it to New York East. Few would be displeased that this never saw the light of day.

1 | Northern Brooklyn

Bushwick, Greenpoint, Williamsburg

A map of Northern Brooklyn appears on the following pages.

Williamsburg Stoop Scene, 1970s

Map of the City of
Williamsburgh with part
of Greenpoint, 1852

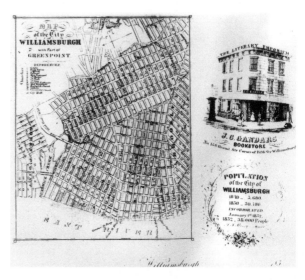

Greenpoint waterfront, 1992

Settled by the Canarsee Indians, Northern Brooklyn was originally known as Cripplebush for the cripplebush or scrub-oak trees that were predominant in the area. Sold to the Dutch West India Company in 1638, the largely swamp-filled region would come to be the preserve of this chapter's three principal neighborhoods: Bushwick, Greenpoint, and Williamsburg.

In 1661, three years prior to New Amsterdam's fall, Governor General Peter Stuyvesant named and helped patent the new town of Boswijck. Dutch for "town in the woods," or as some have argued "heavy woods," it became one of Kings County's six original towns. Arriving at the tail end of the Dutch period, the name had only a brief existence, being anglicized to Bushwick soon after the British takeover.

Topographical considerations were also relevant in the naming of Bushwick's neighbor, Greenpoint. Originally referring to a point of land covered by grass and jutting beyond the shoreline, Greenpoint is said to have been bestowed its name by seventeenth-century sailors who traveled past. The designation was eventually extended to the entire area—today's Greenpoint neighborhood. Though Greenpoint is reputedly the birthplace of the patois "Brooklynese"—a version of the Kings (County) English—no names have been changed to reflect that cultural reality.

Similarly bounded by the East River, Williamsburg was the brainchild of Richard Woodhull, a ferry operator who purchased thirteen acres of Charles Titus's farm in 1802. Woodhull commissioned his friend Col. Jonathan Williams (1750–1815)—U.S. engineer, first superintendent of West Point, and grandnephew to Revolutionary giant Benjamin Franklin—to survey the land. Woodhull honored his comrade by naming Williamsburg after him. Until 1855 the neighborhood had a decisive "h" at the end: Williamsburgh, that is. Yet consolidation into the city of Brooklyn (after a brief period of independence, 1852–55, as a chartered city) stripped the final "h" away. The lost "h" today can be found only on the Williamsburgh Savings

Bank. (For consistency, Williamsburg is written sans "h" in the entries here unless part of a formal name.)

Having absorbed Williamsburg, Greenpoint, and Bushwick in 1855, Brooklyn's size doubled overnight. In its changed configuration, northern Brooklyn for a time took on a different regional name and became known as Brooklyn's Eastern District, in contrast to traditional Brooklyn to its west. The last nomenclatural holdout from that period, Bushwick's Eastern District High-School, succumbed only a few years ago.

Upon incorporation with Brooklyn in 1855, Greenpoint and Bushwick were forced to change some street names to avoid confusion. For example, Henry Street in Greenpoint was changed to North Henry to differentiate it from South Brooklyn's Henry Street. Greenpoint also developed an acrostic naming system with alphabetical and numbered streets, later changed to named ones. Finally, many streets in Williamsburg were renamed to honor signers of the Declaration of Independence.

Ainslie Street James Ainslie was for many years a local judge and school district trustee in Williamsburg. In 1847 Ainslie was counted as one of forty-four persons in the town with a net worth in excess of $10,000.

Anthony Street Possibly named for Susan B(rownell) Anthony (1820–1906), who dedicated her life to the struggle for women's suffrage and other progressive causes. With Elizabeth Cady Stanton and Lucretia Mott, Anthony founded the National Woman's Suffrage Association in 1868. Anthony spoke publicly in Brooklyn quite often. The *Brooklyn Daily Eagle* reported her affirming that "a woman is a person, a person is a citizen and a citizen has a right to vote."

Arion Place Formerly Wall Street, it was renamed after Arion Hall, a nineteenth-century Bushwick concert venue. The associated Arion Society was a choral group and musical society begun by immigrant Germans. In Greek mythology, Arion refers to a seventh-century BC poet and lyre player.

Ash Street Once A Street, the red and white coal ash common to the industrial locale is the probable source for the renaming.

Astral Apartments (184 Franklin Street between India and Java streets) Named for Charles Pratt's Astral Oil Works, these apartments were built in 1885–86 to house Pratt's kerosene refinery workers. *American Architect* wrote that Pratt intended these apartments, known for their model tenement design, for "the widow who has lived in affluence but has been reduced in circumstances," "the shop-girl," "the clerk, or tradesman," and "the great body of first-class mechanics who have

Astral Apartments, 2005

families." Some of the largesse Pratt accrued in the oil business went to financing his eponymous institute in Clinton Hill (see chapter 4).

Banker Street Edward Banker of the ship-chandler firm Schermerhorn, Banker & Company had extensive Greenpoint landholdings in the middle nineteenth century. (Ship chandlers handled some of the accoutrement of sailing ships, like ropes and canvas.) His son, James Hopson Banker, was a vice president of the Bank of New York and close friend of Commodore Cornelius Vanderbilt, with whom he helped establish the New York Central, Harlem, and Lake Shore railroads.

Bartlett Street Dr. Josiah Bartlett (1729–1795) was New Hampshire's first governor, the state's first chief justice, and a signer of the Declaration of Independence. His political achievements came after a successful medical career in which he discovered that Peruvian bark could be used to treat throat distemper. With a homemade remedy, Bartlett also self-diagnosed and cured his own life-threatening feverous condition. Appointed a militia unit commander in 1765, he was soon stripped of his duties because of his strong opposition to royal policy.

Bayard Street Named for Nicholas Bayard (ca. 1644–1707), large landowner, New York mayor, and nephew of Peter Stuyvesant. In the overweening class politics of the day, Bayard's implacable hostility toward the Leislerians in the late 1680s led to his imprisonment, trial for treason, and near hanging. (Populist Jacob Leisler had a brief following in New York in opposition to the wealthy merchants and landowners before he was beheaded.) The incoming colonial governor, Lord Cornbury, overturned the sentence. The street was formerly named Sandford Street, but it was renamed after New York's own Bayard Street.

Bedford Avenue Named for the neighborhood of Bedford Corners (see chapter 4 introduction), Bedford Avenue carries the distinction of being Brooklyn's longest street, extending from Greenpoint to Sheepshead Bay.

Berry Street Dr. Abraham J. Berry

Bedford Avenue and North 9th Street, 1987

(1799–1865) was Williamsburg's first mayor after incorporation as an independent city in 1852. Trained as a physician, Berry was a hero to many for his herculean efforts during the 1832 cholera epidemic. Three decades later, he was surgeon of the 38th New York infantry during the Civil War. Despite being mayor of a newly independent Williamsburg, Berry was a proponent of consolidation with Brooklyn.

Bleecker Street Jan Jansen Bleecker (1641–1732), progenitor of a family of early Dutch settlers residing principally in Albany and New York, came to New Amsterdam at the age of seventeen. Scion Anthony Bleecker, for whom Manhattan's Bleecker Street is named, was a wealthy landowner and shipping merchant, not to mention friend to George Washington and Washington Irving. Bleecker translates from the Dutch as "bleacher of cloth."

Bnos Yakov of Pupa (274 Keap Street) Originally Temple Beth Elohim, this site marks one of the first Jewish congregations in Brooklyn (from 1851). The current occupants of the Ruskinian Gothic place of worship are the Pupa Hasidim, the second-largest ultraorthodox group in Williamsburg after the Satmar. The name translates as "Daughters of Jacob from the town of Pupa, Hungary" ("Papa" in Hungarian). Pupa was once a center for training Orthodox rabbis.

Bogart Street A native of South Holland, Teunis Ghysbertse Bogaerdt (1625–1699) came to settle in Brooklyn's Wallabout area. In 1654 he married Sarah Rapelye, widow of Hans Hansen Bergen and the first European woman born in New Amsterdam. Bogaerdt was one of the trustees and overseers of Brooklyn in the late 1670s. The name was later corrupted to Bogart, and descendents include the prominent American actor Humphrey.

Borinquen Plaza The Taino, Puerto Rico's indigenous people, call their country Borinquen, which translates as "the land of the great lords." Brooklyn's Boricua College, the name referring to one who is Puerto Rican, serves the community with campuses in Williamsburg and Greenpoint.

Brewers Row (North 11th Street between Berry Street and Wythe Avenue) This patch of North 11th Street was named Brewers Row in 2000 to remember the once thriving hops industry in Northern Brooklyn. At the turn of the twentieth century there were nearly fifty breweries in Williamsburg and Bushwick, and Brooklyn produced more beer than Detroit and Milwaukee combined. German immigrants making use of Long Island pure water were the main actors here. The post-prohibition turn toward national-brand brewing spelled the end of such happier (hoppier?) times.

Bridgewater Street Proximity to the former Meeker Avenue (Penny) Bridge that spanned Newtown Creek from Greenpoint to Maspeth resulted in the naming.

Broadway Named for the better-known Broadway across the river, it had been called Division Avenue, which for a time separated Williamsburg from Bushwick.

Bushwick/Hylan Houses (372 Bushwick Avenue) This Williamsburg public housing complex is named for John F. Hylan (1868–1936), two-term New York City mayor from 1918 to 1926. A poor farm boy who "parlayed $1.50 into a comfortable fortune," Hylan became a lawyer and judge and got tapped by the Tammany machine to run for mayor. He was closely identified with the five-cent subway fare and described it as the "cornerstone of the edifice which we call New York City." Tammany turned against him (as did Governor Alfred E. Smith), and he lost his second bid for reelection. Staten Island's north-south spine, Hylan Boulevard, is also named in his honor.

Calhoun Street Likely named for John C. Calhoun (1782–1850), vice president under John Quincy Adams and Andrew Jackson and charismatic Democratic senator from South Carolina. His endorsement of states' rights and the "peculiar institution" of slavery won him allies in the South but kept him from a wider constituency, specifically those alienated by his reactionary sectional loyalty. Arguing that Andrew Jackson's tariff policy benefited the industrial North at the expense of the South, he resigned the vice presidency, the only person ever to do so.

Calyer Street The Calyers were one of the five principal families in early Greenpoint, and Jacobus Calyer (1700–1766) was its patriarch. The present street occupies the spot where the sixty-five-acre Calyer family farm stood from 1766 to 1848. The street was formerly P Street (within Greenpoint's A to Q line), with Calyer Street interrupting the neighborhood's alphabetical patterning.

Clay Street Many attribute the name's origin to Humphrey Clay, an associate of Captain Kidd's, who in 1667 received a land grant on both ends of Meeker Avenue and began a ferry line near the former Penny Bridge. A few, though, have conjectured that it may be named after Henry Clay, the Kentucky senator, secretary of state, and three-time failed presidential nominee who died in 1852, the year the street was opened.

Clymer Street Reared by his uncle after being orphaned at an early age, George Clymer of Philadelphia (1739–1813) represented Pennsylvania at the Continental Congress and signed the Declaration of Independence. After the Revolutionary War, Clymer spent time in the Pennsylvania legislature, where he supported penal code reform and opposed capital punishment. As a member of the U.S. House of Representatives he advocated for closer ties with France and for a liberal naturalization policy.

Cooper Park (Sharon and Olive streets and Maspeth and Morgan avenues) Located in East Williamsburg and named for the noted philanthropist and industrialist Peter Cooper (1791–1883). In 1838 Cooper set up a glue factory on Maspeth Avenue in Brooklyn after relocating from Manhattan's Kip's Bay. He eventually sold the factory to family members in 1865; thirty years later they turned over the grounds to the city of Brooklyn for $55,000, and within a year the site became Cooper Park. Peter Cooper was also an inventor responsible for the *Tom Thumb* (the first) steam locomotive and for patenting the manufacture of gelatin. (The patent was sold fifty years later and used to produce Jell-O.) In Manhattan, Cooper established Cooper Union for the Advancement of Science and Art, one of the country's first free higher-educational institutions.

Statue of Peter Cooper
in front of Cooper Union, 1901

Decatur Street At the tender age of twenty, Steven Decatur (1779–1820) had already become an acting navy lieutenant, later distinguishing himself in the War of 1812. He famously declared, "Our country! In her intercourse with foreign nations may she always be in the right; but our country right or wrong." In 1818, U.S. Capitol architect Benjamin Henry Latrobe finished Decatur's Washington, D.C., home—one of the city's oldest (it's a museum today). Decatur had little time to enjoy it, dying two years after its completion, the result of a duel.

Division Avenue This avenue defined the boundary between the cities of Brooklyn and Williamsburg.

Driggs Avenue Named for Edmund Driggs (d. 1891) the last village president of Williamsburg before its incorporation as a city. Driggs was also a First Ward alderman, president of the Williamsburg City Fire Insurance Company, and a delegate to the 1860 Democratic National Convention in Chicago that nominated Stephen Douglas.

Dunham Place Laid in 1850 and named for David Dunham (ca. 1790–1823), a New York merchant who helped initiate an early steam ferry from Brooklyn to New York, which earned him the nickname "Father of Williamsburg." Dunham was an indefatigable advocate for steam navigation and a pioneer of steamship travel, venturing to Havana, New Orleans, and several southern states. He died a tragic death when he fell overboard in the Hudson River and drowned near West Point while returning —by steamship, of course—from Albany.

Eberhard Faber Pencil Buildings (37 and 61 Greenpoint Avenue; 59 Kent Street) Coming to America in 1848, Eberhard Faber (1822–1879) established a German import business that included pencils. Thirteen years later, on the site of the present United Nations building, he started his own factory with the first mass-produced eraser-tipped pencils. Destroyed by fire in 1872, the firm moved to

Eberhard Faber, 1922

Greenpoint, where it became the world's largest pencil company. It removed to Wilkes-Barre, Pennsylvania, in 1956.

Eckford Street A member of the nineteenth century's foremost shipbuilding families, Eckford Webb (1825–1893) was a founder, in 1850, of the Greenpoint shipyard Webb & Bell at West and Green streets. Webb & Bell was responsible for the extraordinary wood caissons that have kept the Brooklyn Bridge from sinking into the East River. When completed, the caissons were hauled four miles downstream from the Webb & Bell shipyard. Webb Avenue in the Bronx honors the shipbuilder's naval architect father.

Ellery Street An active member of the Rhode Island Sons of Liberty, William Ellery (1727–1820) was a delegate at the 1776 Continental Congress and a signer of the Declaration of Independence. He later reminisced: "I was determined to see how they all looked as they signed what might be their death warrant." Upon retirement he received an appointment from George Washington to serve as the U.S. Customs Collector for the District of Newport. During these years he became outspoken in his desire to abolish slavery from the country.

Evergreen Avenue This avenue serves as the main road leading to Bushwick's Cemetery of the Evergreens, hence the name.

Flushing Avenue This road once led to the town of Flushing, and its name is an anglicization of *Vlissingen* (the name of a Dutch city). The town was historically central to the early struggles, led by John Bowne, over freedom of conscience.

Franklin Street Perhaps the most prominent American of his time, Benjamin Franklin's (1706–1790) achievements are legion, whether as diplomat, inventor, journalist, or statesman. Of the fifty-six signers of the Declaration of Independence, he was the oldest at the age of seventy. A true autodidact with little formal schooling, he practiced what he posited, namely, that "the doors to wisdom are never shut." Williamsburg is named for his surveyor grandnephew, Jonathan Williams.

Gerry Street Elbridge Gerry (1744–1814) was a member of the Continental Congress, a signer of the Declaration of Independence, and governor of Massachusetts. Gerry's concern that individual and states' rights were being insufficiently protected in the early debates over the Constitution led to their inclusion in the Bill of Rights. During his second gubernatorial term, Gerry's party redistricted the state in the hope of winning the next election. Rearranged in a salamander-like shape, the redistricting gave birth to the term "gerrymandering" (from "Gerry" and "salamander"), which defined the partisan practice of boundary manipulation. Gerry later succeeded George Clinton as James Madison's vice president.

Graham Avenue John and James Lorimer Graham were land-jobbers in Williamsburg during the first part of the nineteenth century. Jobbers, whose reputations were less than savory, sought to purchase land not for cultivation or settlement but for the sole purpose of turning a profit.

Grand Ferry Park (between Grand Street, West River Street, and the East River) Named for the Grand Street Ferry, the East River crossing that made its way from Williamsburg to Manhattan. The ferry continued service until 1918, by which time the Williamsburg Bridge had already been servicing pedestrians and vehicles for fifteen years.

Grand Street, 1989

Grattan Street Named in 1888 for Henry Grattan (1746–1820), a Protestant member of the Irish Parliament who valiantly fought for Ireland's independence and the civil and political rights of Catholics. Grattan's support for decolonization was broad: when British troops left Ireland to fight in the American Revolution, Grattan's sympathies extended to the colonists. Though the last two decades of the eighteenth century in Ireland were considered "Grattan's Parliament," he was unable to forestall the inevitable: the 1800 Act of Union that merged the kingdoms of Ireland and Great Britain.

Greenpoint Avenue One of two exceptions to the alphabetical patterning of streets in the neighborhood, Greenpoint Avenue was originally L Street. It became Lincoln Street, then Greenpoint Avenue, then later National Avenue, and finally back to Greenpoint Avenue.

Guernsey Street Thought to be named for Dr. Egbert Guernsey (1823–1903), an early and important practitioner of homeopathic medicine and author of the *Gentleman's Handbook of Homeopathy.* Guernsey's adoption of homeopathic methods led to rebuke from various establishment groups, but his enormous success in the new science was transformative. In addition to his presidency at New York's Metropolitan Hospital (on Blackwell Island, today Roosevelt Island), Guernsey was a founder of the *Williamsburgh Daily Times* (later *Brooklyn Daily Times*) and of the well-regarded monthly medical journal the *New York Medical Times.* He was a large man, often weighing in excess of four hundred pounds.

Guernsey Street, taken from the corner of Norman Avenue, ca. 1992

Harrison Avenue Born into a political family, Virginian Benjamin Harrison (1726–1791) held a variety of offices and was a signer of the Declaration of Independence. He was also no stranger to black humor: when discussion raged about the dangers of being hanged for signing the Declaration, the rotund Harrison reportedly counseled the slight Elbridge Gerry, "I shall have all the advantage over you. It will be all over in a minute for me, but you will be kicking in the air half an hour after I am gone." Harrison's son, William Henry Harrison, went on to become U.S. president.

Hart Street New Jersey farmer John Hart (ca. 1713–1779) was a delegate to the Continental Congress and a signer of the Declaration of Independence. During the Revolutionary War, Hessian mercenaries destroyed Hart's 380-acre farm, and the resultant trauma was central to his wife's illness and eventual death. Once he learned that the British sought to capture him, Hart spent a year hiding out in forests and caves.

Hausman Street Possibly named for Charles Housman (various spellings exist), whose wife, Ariantje, was the daughter of Dirck "the Norman" Volckertsen (see Norman Avenue entry in this chapter).

Havemeyer Street Brothers Frederick C. Havemeyer (1774–1841) and William Havemeyer (1770–1851) were major industrialists who made their money in sugar processing. Arriving from Germany at the turn of the nineteenth century, they soon built a sugar refinery on Vandam Street in Manhattan. William's son, William F. (1804–1874), took over the family business in the 1830s but ventured into politics and became a three-term New York mayor. Cousin Frederick C. Havemeyer Jr. (1807–1891) stayed in the sugar trade and in 1857 established the longstanding South 3rd Street factory on the Williamsburg waterfront. His son, Henry Havemeyer (1847–1907), named the company Domino's Sugar in the early 1900s and worked to corner the market. His Sugar Refineries Company, or "Sugar Trust," functioned like Standard Oil —monopolistically (and like Standard Oil did battle with the government over market

William Frederick Havemeyer, mid-nineteenth century

control). An era ended in 2004 when Domino's Sugar terminated its refining operations and the East River plant (and classic signage) bearing its name. The company is now a part of the British concern Tate & Lyle.

Hewes Street Originally from New Jersey, Declaration of Independence signer Joseph Hewes (1730–1779) moved to North Carolina, made a fortune in the shipping trade, and was elected to be a representative at the Continental

Congress. Though Quaker, he promoted the fight against Great Britain and ultimately broke with the Society of Friends because of their opposition to the war.

Heyward Street Thomas Heyward Jr. of South Carolina (1746–1809) signed the Declaration of Independence at the age of thirty but resigned from the Continental Congress to be a judge in his home state. When the British captured Charleston in 1780, Heyward was imprisoned with fellow South Carolina signers Edward Rutledge and Arthur Middleton for one year in St. Augustine, Florida. The British expropriated his slaves and sold them to sugar planters in Jamaica.

Himrod Street J. S. (John Sutphen) Himrod (1812–1882) was the first minister of the South Bushwick Reformed Church on Bushwick Avenue and (what became) Himrod Street, serving there from 1854 to 1859.

Hooper Street Originally from Boston, Declaration of Independence signer William Hooper (1742–1790) moved to North Carolina after law school and participated in the colonial legislature and Continental Congress. His sharp words against the king led to his disbarment.

Humboldt Street Named for Alexander von Humboldt (1769–1859), a hugely influential naturalist, explorer, and anthropologist whose work in the fields of contemporary meteorology and geography led Darwin to describe him as "the greatest scientific traveler who ever lived." In 1804, following an enormously successful five-year expedition around South America (later recounted in no less than thirty volumes), he came to the United States, befriended Thomas Jefferson, and lectured for several months around the country. Humboldt was gay and left all his personal belongings to his partner, his servant Siefert. His sister later torched all his love letters. He is remembered in the United States via a river, a reservoir, a salt marsh, and a university, as well as lakes, mountains, parks, counties, and towns.

Alexander von Humboldt, mid-nineteenth century

India Street Similar to India House, the private Manhattan clubhouse named to reflect the upsurge in trade to the East, India Street, opened in 1852, sought its own Orientalist connotation.

Ingraham Street Likely named for Duncan Nathaniel Ingraham (1802–1891), a naval officer and large slaveholder best known for defending and freeing Martin Koszta, the Hungarian American kidnapped in Turkey in 1853. He became a midshipman at the advanced age of ten and joined the Confederate Navy five decades later, commanding Charleston Station from 1862 to 1865.

Irving Avenue Born in New York the youngest of eleven children and named after George Washington, Washington Irving (1783–1859) was the author of the short stories "The Legend of Sleepy Hollow" and "Rip Van Winkle" and the comic 1809 novel *The History of New York*. The novel features Dietrich Knickerbocker, whose name is the eponym for the term referring to a descendent of early Dutch settlers. Fittingly, Knickerbocker Avenue (see entry in this chapter) runs parallel to this street.

Java Street Formerly J Street, it was likely renamed to offer exotic illustration of the waterfront cargo—coffee and spices—unloaded here.

Johnson Avenue Of Dutch stock, General Jeremiah Johnson (1766–1852) was a longstanding politician in Brooklyn, first as a trustee and county supervisor and later as the city's third mayor from 1837 to 1838. A vocal champion of Brooklyn's independent metropolitan status, Johnson inflamed New York politicians advocating consolidation. "Between New York and Brooklyn there is nothing in common, either in object, interest or feeling," he once said, "unless it be the waters that flow between them. And even those waters, however frequently passed, must forever continue to form an insurmountable obstacle to their union." Johnson was a brigadier general in the War of 1812, commanding troops stationed at Fort Greene, and was also an early historian of Brooklyn.

Keap Street This street's origin is an oddity. It is named for Thomas McKean of Pennsylvania (1734–1817), the final signer of the Declaration of Independence, but his scrawled signature on the document led to the street name's Williamsburg bastardization.

Kent Avenue/Kent Street Prominent jurist James Kent (1763–1847) was the first professor of law at Columbia College. Appointed in 1793 on the recommendation of John Jay, he taught for only three years but returned following his retirement from the New York Court of Chancery. Kent's *Commentaries on American Law* (4 vols., 1826–30), the product of his celebrated Columbia lectures, mark the onset of modern legal scholarship.

Kingsland Avenue Ambrose Cornelius Kingsland (1804–1878), Whig mayor of New York for one term (1851–53), was also a widely known Greenpoint resident and developer, not to mention sperm whale oil merchant. With Samuel J. Tilden (see chapter 5), Kingsland purchased a large swathe of Greenpoint's surveyed land. Despite a corruption-riddled mayoralty, Kingsland performed one major public service: the appropriation of funds for what would become Central Park.

Knickerbocker Avenue Received its name from the Washington Irving character Dietrich Knickerbocker (see Irving Avenue entry in this chapter).

Kossuth Place Revered as the "father of Hungarian democracy," Lajos Kossuth (pronounced "Kosh-shoot") (1802–1894) was a hero of the 1848 revolution and governor of Hungary during its struggle for independence. Despite

Austrian and Russian suppression, Hungary later received partial autonomy within a newly renamed Austro-Hungarian Empire. In 1851–52 Kossuth toured the United States, where he became the first formally invited foreign dignitary since Lafayette to speak before the House of Representatives.

Lajos Kossuth, 1849

Lee Avenue This avenue honors two fraternal Virginia signers of the Declaration of Independence: Richard Henry Lee (1732–1794) and Francis Lightfoot Lee (1734–1797). Though a slaveholder himself, the first piece of legislation Richard Henry Lee introduced in the Virginia House of Burgesses recommended levying an extraordinary tax on anyone importing slaves "to put an end to that iniquitous and disgraceful traffic within the colony of Virginia." Six years later, the brothers denounced the Stamp Act and threatened colonists who honored it in one of the first significant acts of sedition against the king. Lee Avenue is today Williamsburg's central Hasidic commercial artery.

Leonard Street Possibly named for John Leonard, a commissioner assigned with laying out streets in Bushwick after the town's partial 1835 annexation to Williamsburg.

Lindsay Triangle (Throop Avenue, Broadway, Lorimer and Middleton streets)

Named for two-term New York mayor John V(liet) Lindsay (1921–2000), a liberal Republican from the East Side's silk stocking district. Lindsay's administration embodied the free-wheeling, countercultural, civil rights–focused politics of the 1960s and strove to humanize New York through progressive policies designed to support minorities and the poor. The absence in New York of the kind of riots that engulfed cities like Newark or Detroit at the end of the decade can partially be attributed to Lindsay's concerted attention to inner-city dynamics. Ultimately, bureaucracy, mismanagement, and a misunderstanding of the outer boroughs damaged his tenure in office, and a quixotic 1972 presidential campaign on the Democrat ticket went nowhere. Lindsay was a tragic figure in New York politics, one who sought to bring government to the people but ended up mired in some of its worst inefficiencies.

John Lindsay, 1966

Lorimer Street Lorimer comes from the maiden name of the mother of John and James Lorimer Graham (see Graham Avenue entry in this chapter).

Lynch Street Thomas Lynch Jr. (1749–1779) of South Carolina was a signer of the Declaration of Independence but had to resign from the Continental Congress in 1776 because of illness. In an effort to restore therapeutically his failing health, he and his wife left for the West Indies in 1779, but their vessel was lost at sea.

Manhattan Avenue William Tooker's classic 1901 essay "The Origin of the Name Manhattan" translates the Delaware Indian name as "island of hills." The street had been called Ewen Avenue in the Williamsburg section (for the surveyor Daniel Ewen) and Orchard Street and Union Avenue in Greenpoint. By 1897, though, it was Manhattan Avenue throughout.

Maujer Street Named for Daniel Maujer (ca. 1809–1882), a lawyer and alderman of the Fifteenth Ward. Maujer was born in Guernsey in the Channel Islands, came to the United States at the age of eighteen, and moved to Williamsburg in 1840. He was a long-term member of the Brooklyn Board of Education, including a period as its president. In 1859 Maujer was also one of the commissioners appointed to create a Brooklyn equivalent to New York's Central Park. Prospect Park was the result of the commissioners' negotiations.

McCarren Park Born in East Cambridge, Massachusetts, and named for the Revolutionary patriot Patrick Henry, state senator Patrick Henry McCarren

McCarren Park, ca. 1997

(1847–1909) was one of Brooklyn's most powerful Democratic Party leaders. Best known for spearheading the legislative fight for the construction of Brooklyn's second East River crossing, the Williamsburg Bridge, McCarren was no stranger to corruption and became an ally to monopolies like Standard Oil and the Sugar Trust. An ongoing nemesis of Tammany Hall and Tammany leader Charles Murphy, he drew the machine's ire by opposing William Randolph Hearst's 1908 gubernatorial run. Outside of Henry Ward Beecher's, McCarren's funeral was the most significant (of its time) in Brooklyn.

McGuinness Boulevard Greenpoint Democratic leader Peter J. McGuinness (1888–1948) was often called the "First Citizen of Greenpoint" and was a tireless advocate of what he saw as the beauties of the neighborhood. McGuinness called the industrial area, apparently without irony, the "Garden Spot of the Universe." He began his political career as an alderman, during which time he proposed a city ordinance to ban women from smoking in public (it failed). He later took on the reins of party boss and testified in the celebrated Seabury investigation, which led to Mayor Jimmy Walker's resignation in 1932. "Greenpoint has not only given and given to the nation, but she has given good," McGuinness once observed, "and when history is wrote and re-wrote, Greenpoint is going to have its share of credit."

McKibbin Street John S. McKibbin purchased part of Jacob Boerum's farm and opened this street in 1853 with his partner, Thomas Nicholls. The street and surrounding area were home to a large number of German settlers, leading to its informal designation: "Dutchtown" (Deutschtown).

Meeker Avenue Attorney Samuel M. Meeker (1820–1891), Williamsburg's corporation counsel, drafted the charter for the newly independent city in 1851. He also helped establish the Williamsburgh Savings Bank that year and later became its president.

Menahan Street Named for Patrick J. Menahan, whose corset manufacturing business existed here in the early 1880s, when the street was still called Ralph Street.

Meserole Avenue/Meserole Street The Meseroles were one of Greenpoint's original five families. Having arrived from France in 1663, Jan Meserole (d. 1695) acquired land from his father-in-law, Pieter Praa (one of Greenpoint's first European settlers), land that his sons Jacob and Abraham later settled. Abraham Meserole was the one who suggested the street be named after the family.

Middleton Street Arthur Middleton (1742–1787) came from a wealthy slaveholding planter family and was one of four South Carolina signers of the Declaration of Independence. Educated in England, he was nonetheless a fierce critic of British rule. With fellow signers Edward Rutledge and Thomas Heyward Jr. (see respective entries), he was imprisoned in St.

Augustine, Florida, after the British took Charleston in 1780. Today, his family's estate, Middleton Place in South Carolina, a National Historic Landmark, is an authentically preserved nineteenth-century plantation (minus the slave labor) with the oldest landscaped gardens in the country.

Monitor Street One of Greenpoint's major historical claims is that John Ericsson's 1862 ironclad USS *Monitor* was produced at the local Continental Iron Works. Participating in the Battle of Hampton Roads, the first naval fight between ironclad warships (previously ships were made largely of wood), the *Monitor* fought the Confederate's ship *Virginia* to a draw. From then on, naval warfare changed profoundly. The *Monitor* eventually sank off the North Carolina coast in December 1862 and was located only in 1973.

Monsignor McGolrick Park Originally Winthrop Park, it was renamed in 1941 for Monsignor Edward J. McGolrick (1857–1938), pastor of St. Cecilia's Church on Herbert Street. Appointed in November 1888 by John Loughlin, Brooklyn's first bishop, McGolrick presided over a dramatic increase in the wealth and resources of the church.

Moore Street Thomas C. Moore was a local Williamsburg manufacturer of netting and wire sieves.

Morgan Avenue Likely named for the Morgan brothers, surveyors who were active in the mid- to late nineteenth century throughout Northern Brooklyn.

Moultrie Street William Moultrie of South Carolina (1730–1805) had a highly respected military career as a colonel and general in the Continental Army. He defended Charleston against the British in 1776 but was later taken prisoner when it fell in 1780. He was released two years later in a prisoner exchange with the British general John Burgoyne. After the war, Moultrie served several terms as governor and was responsible for moving the state capital from Charleston to Columbia.

Noble Street Named for James Noble, a trustee of the village of Williamsburg prior to its independence and later consolidation.

Norman Avenue The first European to settle in Greenpoint, in 1645, Dirck Volckertsen was nicknamed "the Norman," a none-too-subtle reference to his Scandinavian origins. A ship carpenter, he received a patent from the Dutch for a large section of today's Greenpoint and built a house on the corner of Calyer and Franklin streets. He sold much of the land to Jacob Hay in 1653, though he remained in Bushwick. Bushwick Creek was once known as Norman's Creek.

Penn Street A lawyer and one of three North Carolina signers of the Declaration of Independence, John Penn (1741–1788) served on his state's Board of War with the responsibility of ensuring sufficient supplies to the militia.

Peter Luger Steak House (178 Broadway) The steakhouse has been a fixture in Williamsburg since 1887, when it opened as Charles Luger's Café, Billiards, and Bowling Alley. Originally located at Driggs Avenue and South 8th

Street, it moved to 178 Broadway in 1904. Peter Luger (1866–1941) was a German-born restaurateur who also owned an establishment on Sunrise Highway in Valley Stream, New York. His nephew, Carl Luger, was the Brooklyn chef for forty years.

Powers Street William P. Powers worked as a clerk in the offices of the Graham brothers (see entry in this chapter). Powers became a landowner in name only: in order for the Grahams to facilitate a specific land transaction, Powers was made a nominal proprietor of 939 lots.

Provost Street Another of the original Greenpoint families, Huguenot David Provost (sometimes spelled Provoost) arrived in New Amsterdam in 1634 and became Brooklyn's first constable. His son was mayor of New York from 1699 to 1700.

Richardson Street A Williamsburg founding father, Lemuel Richardson was on the board of directors of the first Bank of Williamsburg and owned a rope-walk (a place where rope is made) in the area.

Roberto Clemente Plaza (64 Division Avenue) Pittsburgh Pirates right fielder Roberto Clemente (1934–1972) played eighteen seasons, winning the National League's batting championship four times and being chosen League MVP in 1966 and World Series MVP in 1971. On New Year's Eve 1972 he flew to earthquake-stricken Nicaragua with medical and food supplies, enraged that previous shipments never made it there. He died when his plane crashed off the coast of his native Puerto Rico. Clemente is the first Latino inducted into baseball's Hall of Fame.

Rodney Street America's second-smallest state has one of its favorite sons, Caesar Rodney (1728–1784), honored in central Williamsburg. A Delaware native, Rodney was a member of the Stamp Act Congress, a delegate to the Continental Congress, a brigadier general of the Delaware militia, and fourth president of the state of Delaware (during the period of the Articles of Confederation, states had presidents). When he was Speaker of the Delaware Assembly, Rodney tried unsuccessfully to pass a law blocking the further importation of slaves.

Roebling Street After studying philosophy with no less an authority than Hegel, Prussian design engineer John Augustus Roebling (1806–1869) came to the United States seeking ways to marry the material and the spiritual. Spanning the fields of metaphysics and engineering, bridge building at the time was an enterprise that spoke directly to considerations of aesthetics, reason, and science. Drawing out the Hegelian motif in Roebling's thinking, Alan Trachtenberg observed, "Brooklyn Bridge was in its creator's mind a principle of order. Representing nature's laws and man's history, the bridge subdued, in mind if not in fact, the implied chaos of millions of people making their separate ways across the river. It would give their passage a form, and link them in consciousness to their national destinies as Americans." The suspension bridge, which Roebling revolutionized, was for him the product of such thinking.

After designing and surveying the site for the bridge, Roebling suffered a fatal accident, and his son, Washington Roebling (1837–1926), took over the project and added various important design improvements. Washington oversaw the bridge's construction until stricken with "the bends," a disease catalyzed by working in the massive caissons. An invalid, he still directed the work on the bridge from his 110 Columbia Heights window, though it was a third Roebling, Washington's wife, Emily (1843–1903), who, teaching herself civil engineering, carried forth the on-site supervision through opening day in 1883.

Ross Street A lawyer, Tory, and Crown Prosecutor, Pennsylvanian George Ross (1730–1779) was not an obvious choice to become a Continental Congress delegate and, ultimately, a signer of the Declaration of Independence. Flag designer Betsy Ross was the wife of his nephew.

Rush Street Benjamin Rush (1745–1813), a chemist and signer of the Declaration of Independence, was one of the country's most acclaimed physicians and a man of some paradox: in the forefront of the care for the mentally ill, he also taught the disavowed practice of bloodletting. Politically there was little ambiguity to his positions. Rush stood at the center of the day's progressive politics, adamantly opposing slavery and capital punishment and supporting free public schooling and better quality education for women.

Rutledge Street Attorney Edward Rutledge (1749–1800) was the youngest signer of the Declaration of Independence. After the Revolution, Rutledge served as a representative in the U.S. Congress and then as governor of South Carolina until his death.

St. Barbara's Catholic Church (138 Bleecker Street) Built in 1910, St. Barbara's is one of Brooklyn's tallest buildings. The church was named for the daughter of local brewer Leonard Eppig, a major contributor to the church.

St. Stanislaus Kostka's School (12 Newel Street) St. Stanislaus Kostka (1550–1568) was born to a Polish noble family and beatified by Pope Paul V in 1605.

Scholes Street James Scholes in 1831 purchased the land where the street lies from the heirs of Jeremiah Remsen.

Seigel Street Named for Franz Sigel (1824–1902) (an "e" was added to the street name), a

Franz Sigel, ca. 1861

refugee from the 1848 revolutions in Europe who became a journalist, superintendent of St. Louis's public school system, and later brigadier and major general in the Civil War. Though he eventually lost his military command, he was famous for recruiting German Americans to abolitionism and the union struggle.

Stanwix Street English general John Stanwix (ca. 1690–1765) fought in the Seven Years War and helped build what was later named Fort Stanwix, now a national monument in Rome, New York.

Stephen A. Rudd Playground (Bushwick Avenue, Aberdeen Street, and Granite Street) After receiving a law degree at the age of forty and then working as Police Department secretary during the mayoralty of his friend John Hylan, Stephen A. Rudd (1874–1936) served fourteen years as a Brooklyn Democratic alderman and then as U.S. congressman representing the areas of Bushwick and East New York.

Stockholm Street Named for two landholding brothers, Andrew and Abraham Stockholm, who provided six lots of land on Bushwick Avenue for the building of the Second Dutch Reformed Church of South Bushwick in the early 1850s. The church's first pastor was John S. Himrod (see entry in this chapter).

Suydam Street An important Dutch family and one of Brooklyn's oldest, the Suydams owned a farm that comprised a large section of Bushwick. For several centuries before it was razed in 1899 the family's Bushwick homestead stood on Evergreen Avenue and Madison Street. The Suydam's original ancestor is probably Hendrick Rycken, whose children were said to adopt the name Suydam for "South of the Dam" (*suyt-dam* in Dutch). They also had property in what was then the town of Bedford, and there is a Suydam Place today in Crown Heights.

Taylor Street Irish-born George Taylor (1716–1781) was a Pennsylvania signer of the Declaration of Independence, a member of the Committee of Correspondence, and a businessman with a profitable iron concern. Though a wealthy slaveowner, he became heavily indebted later in life.

Ten Eyck Street Originally of Moers, Lowlands Germany, Coenraedt Ten Eyck (1617–1686) immigrated in 1651 to New Amsterdam. Coenties Slip in Manhattan, where he lived, comes from a contraction of his own name and that of his second wife, Antje. He had many descendents, including William Ten Eyck, a deacon at the Second Dutch Reformed Church of South Bushwick.

Thornton Street New Hampshire signer of the Declaration of Independence, physician Matthew Thornton (1714–1803) was a leading citizen and landholder in Londonderry responsible for writing the first state constitution.

Union Avenue Unlike Union Street (see chapter 3), the name of this Northern Brooklyn street has as its referent the Civil War.

Van Dam Street From a prominent New York family during the colonial period, Rip Van Dam (ca. 1660–1749) was briefly acting colonial governor (1731–32) before William Cosby. Once Cosby took the reins, Van Dam would anger his successor by vocally defending newspaper editor John Peter Zenger, whom Cosby claimed had slandered him. Rip Van Dam was also the owner of the building on Nassau Street in Manhattan where the New Theatre put on the first professional play in North America, George Farquhar's comedy "The Recruiting Officer." Manhattan's Van Dam Street is named for Rip Van Dam's grandson Anthony, a city alderman and Tory who fled to London after the Revolutionary War.

Varick Avenue/Varick Street Richard Varick (1753–1831) served under General Philip Schuyler during the Revolutionary War's Battle of Saratoga before moving to West Point and becoming aide-de-camp to Benedict Arnold. Implicated in Arnold's treason by association, Varick was arrested but eventually cleared. He later became private secretary to George Washington and mayor of New York from 1791 to 1801. Varick Street in Manhattan also bears his name.

Wallabout Street The name comes from a corruption of the Dutch *Waal Bocht,* meaning "Walloon Bay" or "Bay of Foreigners." This small Williamsburg street is the only remaining identifying marker of the once thriving early waterfront area. The name was variously employed throughout Brooklyn's history: initially a village bordering the water, then the name of the bay, and later that of a well-known neighborhood wholesale produce exchange market. During the American Revolution, Wallabout Bay was the site of the nightmarish prison ships that took the lives of some 11,500 Americans (see Prison Ship Martyrs' Monument, chapter 4).

Walton Street Originally from Virginia, George Walton (1741–1804) moved to Georgia and became a delegate to the Continental Congress and a signer of the Declaration of Independence. During the Battle of Savannah in 1778, he was captured and later freed through a prisoner exchange. Following the war, Walton served as Georgia's chief justice, governor, and senator.

Waterbury Street Born in Groton Falls, Connecticut, Noah Waterbury (d. 1862) became a shoemaker in Brooklyn after moving there at the age of fifteen. He later owned a distillery (on South 2nd Street and then on South 9th Street) and became active in real estate. In 1827, Waterbury was appointed the first president of the village of Williamsburg and later the first president of the Williamsburgh City Bank at its founding in 1852.

Weirfield Street This street is named for local resident Thomas Weirfield, a surveyor active in public affairs.

Whipple Street William Whipple (1730–1785) was a seaman, merchant, New Hampshire delegate to the Continental Congress, and signer of the Declaration of Independence. As a sea captain he was responsible for transporting slaves from the coast of Africa to Portsmouth, and as brigadier general he successfully led the New Hampshire militia against General Burgoyne at Saratoga and Stillwater. Prince Whipple, one of William Whipple's slaves, fought in the Revolutionary War and is the only African American in Emanuel Leutze's classic 1851 painting *Washington Crossing the Delaware.*

Williamsburg Bridge Opened in 1903 and slightly longer than the Brooklyn Bridge, it was called for a time the "New Eastern District Bridge" and the "New East River Bridge."

Wilson Avenue Named for the twenty-eighth president, the street was called Hamburg Avenue until 1918, when anti-German sentiment resulting from World War I led to its renaming.

Wilson Street A leading constitutional lawyer raised in Scotland, James Wilson (1742–1798) was key to breaking Pennsylvania's deadlock at the Second Continental Congress and to getting state approval of the Declaration of Independence. After the war, he was appointed to Philadelphia's Constitutional Convention and in 1789 became a justice of the Supreme Court. Despite his judicial prominence, Wilson was drawn to gambling and profiteering and in the 1790s became involved in an ill-founded scheme to recruit European immigrants to the West. To avoid debtors' prison, he was forced, while remaining associate justice of the Supreme Court, to leave Philadelphia (then the nation's capital) for Burlington, Vermont.

Withers Street Originally from Virginia, Reuben Withers was the proprietor of the Houston Street Ferry. He was involved in China-related trade as part of the firm Withers & Heard and was president of the Bank of the State of New York. Withers married the daughter of David Dunham (see entry in this chapter).

Woodhull Hospital (760 Broadway) Two years after commencing a ferry in 1800 from North 2nd Street to Grand Street, Richard Woodhull began mapping out the farming community then called Cripplebush (see chapter introduction.)

Wythe Avenue/Wythe Place Eminent Virginian lawyer and teacher George Wythe (1726–1806) lived in Williamsburg (Virginia) and was a tutor of Thomas Jefferson. Wythe was a signer of the Declaration of Independence and upon the war's conclusion became a professor of law at the College of William and Mary. Wythe was still active at the age of eighty-one, when he was poisoned with arsenic-laced coffee by, most suspect, his grandnephew.

2 | Downtown Brooklyn

Brooklyn Heights, Downtown–City Center, DUMBO, Fulton Ferry, Vinegar Hill

A map of Downtown Brooklyn appears on the following pages.

Down Under the Manhattan Bridge Overpass (DUMBO), 1995

Fulton Ferry Landing, late 1980s

Downtown Brooklyn, 1942

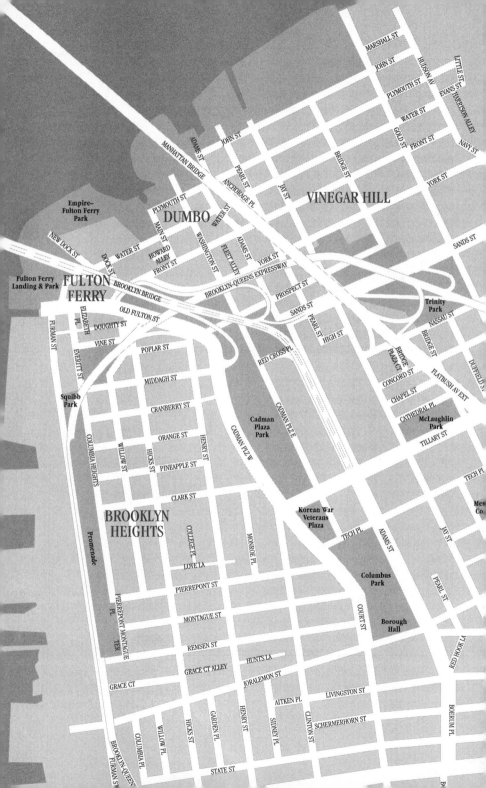

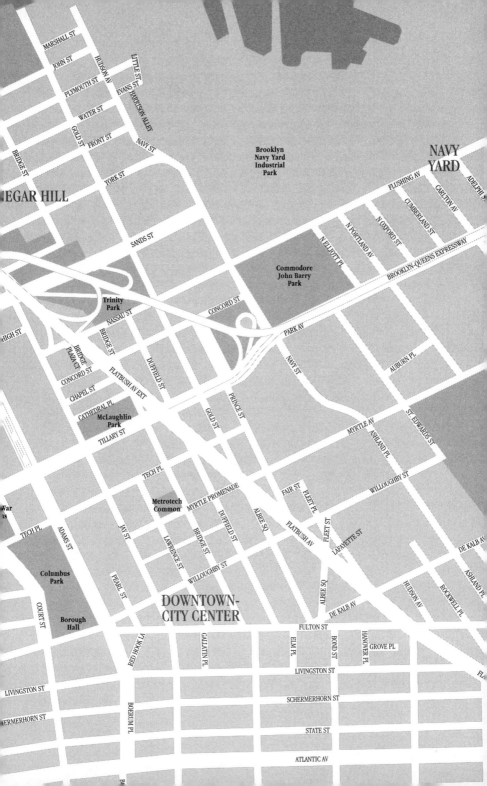

AMunsee Delaware speaking group, the Marechkawieck were the earliest known inhabitants in the neighborhoods covered in this chapter, an area that conforms to the town of Breukelen's original boundaries. With their flight, a function of war and subjugation, Dutch settlements were built along the waterfront and became known as the Wallabout.

From a corruption of the Dutch *Waal Bocht,* meaning "Bay of Foreigners" or "Walloon Bay" (Walloons being inhabitants of an area in Belgium), the name likely derives from a Walloon, Joris Rapelye, one of Brooklyn's earliest European immigrants who secured his land through a Dutch West India Company patent. John Jackson and his brothers in 1781 purchased the property from Rapelye's descendents, and they in turn were bought out two decades later by the U.S. Navy, who established the New York Naval Shipyard, the official name of the Brooklyn Navy Yard.

In the early nineteenth century, immigration redefined the area's demographics. Vinegar Hill, east of the Manhattan Bridge anchorage, offers a case in point. A public-relations gambit by John Jackson to recruit new residents from the influx of Irish newcomers, the name is drawn from the 1798 Battle of Vinegar Hill in Wexford County, Ireland, in which Irish rebels were defeated in a clash with the English. By the middle of the century nearly half of Vinegar Hill's residents were Irish, many of them dockworkers at the Navy Yard, and the neighborhood was informally called "Irish Town."

In the shadow of the Brooklyn Bridge stands today's Fulton Ferry section, immortalized in Walt Whitman's classic 1856 poem "Crossing Brooklyn Ferry." Once simply "The Ferry" (*Het Veer* in Dutch), it was the departure site of Cornelius Dircksen's 1642 ferry, the first to traverse the river. This medium of transport, even in the pre-steam age, led to the development of the area and its key role in Brooklyn proper. Robert Fulton's radical nineteenth-century innovation accelerated those trends exponentially.

Turning inland, Brooklyn Heights, whose name refers to the bluffs over the waterfront on which this neighborhood was built, is considered New York City's first suburban community. Originally called Clover Hill, underscoring the bucolic nature of this longtime rural area, the Heights was developed in the early nineteenth century in large part through the efforts of Hezekiah Pierrepont, who sought to create an exclusive suburban oasis. The area had been dominated by a small group of landowning families—including the Middaghs, Remsens, and Hickses—evidenced by the streets that bear their names.

Immediately to the north, DUMBO, named literally for its location "Down Under the Manhattan Bridge Overpass," spans the industrial neighborhood between Main and Bridge streets. The acronym is attributed to artists who conceived the name in the 1970s. The site of a thriving manufacturing area, DUMBO has in the past been home to Antoine Zerega's macaroni factory, thought to be the first pasta factory in America; the Arbuckle Company, whose claim to fame was packed coffee in bags; and Robert Gair's firm, which produced folding paper boxes.

Adams Street Originally Congress Street, it was renamed by Port Collector Joshua Sands (see entry in this chapter) after second U.S. president John Adams (1735–1826), who nominated Sands to his post. Before the nation's capital moved to Philadelphia, Adams served as Washington's vice president in New York.

Aitken Place Native Brooklynite Monsignor Ambrose S. Aitken (ca. 1889–1959) was a pastor in several Brooklyn and Long Island churches prior to his eighteen-year affiliation with St. Charles Borromeo Roman Catholic Church (on Sidney Place). The street was named in 1960.

Anchorage Place Anchorage Place may relate to the once prominent shipping trade along the East River or to the anchoring cables of the Manhattan Bridge, which was under construction when the street was named.

Bridge Street Intended as the site for an East River crossing, it instead ended up smack between two others: the Manhattan and Brooklyn bridges.

Brooklyn Borough Hall (209 Joralemon Street)

Built on land sold for $53,000 by the Pierreponts and Remsens, Borough Hall was originally called City Hall at its completion in 1848. The name was downgraded when Brooklyn lost its independent metropolitan status a half century later.

In the annals of lost Brooklyn names stands Alois Fabry Jr., commissioned in 1937 by the Federal Arts Project of the Works Project Administration (WPA) to paint two monumental nine-hundred-square-foot murals of Brooklyn's history for Borough Hall's central rotunda. One panel illustrated Brooklyn's past

Brooklyn Borough Hall: Brooklyn—Past and Present, 1938

Brooklyn—Past and Present mural study

(1609–1898), spotlighting the usual suspects (Beecher, Whitman) and events (the Battle of Brooklyn, building of the Brooklyn Bridge); the other panel illustrated the postconsolidation period including Floyd Bennett Field and the subway's extension to Brooklyn, elements that reflect Brooklyn's modernization.

After the completion of the murals in 1938/9, Fabry was the target of conservative backlash from politicians and the press and faced rebuke for his alleged "progressive" style and "subversive" content; a figure in the murals that bears some resemblance to Lenin may have played an additional role in the critics' aversion. Armed with Mayor LaGuardia's endorsement, Brooklyn Borough President John Cashmore cast the final blow and forced the murals' removal in 1946. Sixty years later, their whereabouts remain unknown. Eerily reminiscent of the destruction of Diego Rivera's Rockefeller Center mural in 1934, the plight of Fabry's WPA murals is a forgotten stain on the history of Kings County.

Brooklyn Bridge Formally established in 1869 by the New York Bridge Company (composed of New York and Brooklyn board members), the bridge was referred to by several names before its completion, including the "East River Bridge," the "Great East River Bridge," and the "Great Suspension Bridge." Already in 1873 the *New York Tribune* had dubbed it the "Brooklyn Bridge," though this was far from standard. Even on opening day, May 24, 1883, with President Chester Arthur in attendance and over 150,000 persons ready to make the

Brooklyn Bridge

crossing, the bridge was dedicated as "The New York and Brooklyn Bridge" (though the *New York Times* report of the event used "Brooklyn Bridge," asserting that it was "decidedly Brooklyn's celebration"). Not long thereafter, probably due to the boon for Brooklyn that the bridge brought, the swing toward the name Brooklyn Bridge began in full. A Board of Aldermen resolution on January 26, 1915, made it official.

Brooklyn Heights Esplanade/Promenade An esplanade is a raised walkway often designed for recreational purposes and usually near a body of water. While the formal name of this raised walkway covering Orange to Remsen streets and cantilevered over the Brooklyn-Queens Expressway (BQE) is the "Esplanade," it is commonly known as the "Promenade." Dating from 1951

Brooklyn Heights Esplanade/Promenade, 1970s

it is the city's second esplanade/promenade; the first was completed in Manhattan's Carl Schurz Park thirteen years earlier.

Brooklyn Historical Society (128 Pierrepont Street) Established by Henry Pierrepont (1808–1888) as the Long Island Historical Society in 1863, the institution's name was changed in 1985 to reflect more accurately its majority holdings.

Cadman Plaza Born and raised in England, Reverend Dr. Samuel Parkes Cadman (1864–1936) was one of the country's leading ministers and the head of Brooklyn's Central Congregational Church on Hancock Street near Franklin Avenue for thirty-five years. Progressive in orientation, Cadman was famous for his strongly held views, whether attacking the ROTC for "encouraging belief in violence as the final resort in international differences," fulminating against loyalty oaths for teachers—"impertinent interference with academic freedom," or disputing the existence of a fire-and-brimstone hell. Cadman's popularity reached across the country with his noted radio sermons, and he is credited with coining the term "Cathedral of Commerce" to describe the Woolworth Building at its 1913 opening.

Cathedral Place Named for nearby St. James Roman Catholic Church, the seat of the bishop of Brooklyn. Founded by the Irish-born Peter Turner (1787–1863), when built in 1822 it was Long Island's first Roman Catholic church.

Chapel Street Named for the chapel associated with St. James Roman Catholic Church (see Cathedral Place entry above).

Clark Street The street was planned by the Hicks brothers in 1806 and named for Captain William Clark, who set up a ropewalk (a place for manufacturing rope) that traversed Henry and Furman streets.

Clinton Street (see Clinton Avenue, chapter 4)

College Place This street is named for the short-lived Brooklyn Collegiate Institute for Young Ladies, whose nearby four-story (conspicuous for its time) Hicks Street building had its cornerstone laid in 1829 by General Lafayette. At the building's dedication, St. Ann's Church's Reverend Charles McIlvaine emphasized that young women "should be trained to think and be enabled to take the position of intellectual beings wherever they may go." Until its demise a mere thirteen years later, father and son principals Isaac Van Doren and Jacob L. Van Doren sought to provide equal education to women and "afford young ladies the same advantages in acquiring an education that are enjoyed by the other sex in our colleges."

Columbia Heights The Heights refer to the estate of Hezekiah Beers Pierrepont, whose property scenically overlooked the water in the early nineteenth century. His mansion, "Four Chimneys," carried a view (after 1814) of Fulton's landmark steam ferry, for which Pierrepont was an important investor.

Concord Street Most likely named for the historically significant town of Concord, Massachusetts, an early battle site of the Revolutionary War and an inspirational venue for the literary masterpieces of Emerson, Thoreau, and Hawthorne. Walt Whitman's grade school stood on Concord and Adams streets.

Court Street With Brooklyn chartered as a city in 1834, plans for a new city hall were set in motion. Astride the new *hotel de ville,* a court building was to be built on a street renamed for the courthouse. According to plan, in 1835 George Street changed to Court Street, but it took until 1848 for Gamaliel King's Greek Revival City Hall to reach completion. As for the courthouse, it was finished only in 1865 and bypassed Court Street entirely, ending up instead on Joralemon Street (it was torn down in 1952).

Court Street, 1928

Cranberry Street (together with Orange and Pineapple streets) Conventional wisdom today lays the idiosyncratic fruit namings with the Hicks brothers. Local legend is more intriguing: Lady Middagh, in her consternation over solipsistic landowners naming streets for themselves, took the street signs down and replaced them with these. While the city elders were displeased with Middagh's bold act, she convinced the Board of Aldermen to accept the new names. In this telling, it is likely that she also named Willow and Poplar streets.

Doughty Street The street is named for a member of one of Brooklyn's earliest families, Charles Doughty (1759–1844), a lawyer and trustee during the 1816 incorporation of Brooklyn village and later village president. In Brooklyn's first ever act of manumission on record (1797), Doughty freed his twenty-eight-year-old slave Caesar Foster. "Having been largely instrumental in procuring the passage of the emancipation act, by which . . . slavery was abolished in New York state," the *Brooklyn Daily Eagle* recalled decades later, African Americans "used to assemble on the anniversary of emancipation day and proceed to Mr. Doughty's house, carrying turkeys, chickens, ducks and geese in great quantities . . . large enough to give his whole family dyspepsia for a month."

Doughty's life took an unexpected turn when he jettisoned his Quaker past for Swedenborgian theology, named for Emmanuel Swedenborg (1688–1772), who believed that the second coming was already here. Doughty's conversion destroyed his thriving law practice. Never one to duck from controversy, he crossed the river to New York City and spent a number of years as pastor of a Swedenborgian congregation on Pearl Street, where the New York County Courthouse now stands.

Duffield Street Dr. John Duffield of Pennsylvania was a surgeon during the Revolutionary War and later one of Brooklyn's first physicians.

Elizabeth Place Dating from the 1820s the street is possibly named for Elizabeth Cornell; the prominent Cornell family built "Four Chimneys," later the large home of Hezekiah Pierrepont (see Columbia Heights entry in this chapter). George Washington briefly used the premises as his headquarters during the Battle of Brooklyn.

Empire-Fulton Ferry State Park (New Dock Street at Water Street) Named for the postbellum warehouse complex (Empire Stores) that once stocked food items including coffee beans, grains, and sugar. The warehouse is still standing on Water Street (See Fulton Ferry mention in the introduction.)

Evans Street Captain Samuel Evans (d. 1824) worked as Captain Commandant at the nearby Brooklyn Navy Yard. With John Little (see entry in this chapter) he established a ferry that ran from the Navy Yard area to New York.

Everit Street Quaker Thomas Everit and his descendents are the source for this Brooklyn street. The Everits were longstanding butchers who once ran a slaughterhouse on the corner of Fulton and Columbia streets. One can find an additional "t" at the name's end in older maps, but the current spelling is the correct one.

Fleet Place In the mid-seventeenth century, British navy captain Thomas Fleet transported his family on his own boat from England to Huntington, Long Island. Descendent Samuel Fleet (1786–1864), for whom the street is named, was the town's postmaster, local librarian, and principal of Huntington Academy, and published Long Island's first magazine, the *Long Island Jour-*

nal of Philosophy and Cabinet of Variety. A slaveholder, Fleet moved to Brooklyn and became wealthy through farming and property ownership.

Fox Square (Fulton Street and Flatbush Avenue) Built by William Fox of Twentieth Century Fox in 1929, the former four-thousand-seat Fox Theater in the 1950s and 1960s became home to popular rock concerts emceed by Murray "the K" Kaufman. It was demolished in 1970.

Front Street Like Front Streets elsewhere, the street is named descriptively to highlight the fact that it once graced (or "fronted") the waterfront. Landfill changed all that.

Fulton Street Through his steam engine, inventor and engineer Robert Fulton (1765–1815) helped change the landscape of nineteenth-century Brooklyn. Seven years after Fulton's steam-powered *Clermont* sailed from New York to Albany, and 172 years after the first rowboat ferry of Cornelius Dircksen crossed the waters of the East River, Fulton's 1814 *Nassau* steam ferry made the traverse from Brooklyn to New York. Old Fulton Street, part of the original Fulton Street, still stands by the river.

Laid out in 1704, Fulton Street followed the road of the old Kings Highway. By the mid-nineteenth century it became the epicenter of Brooklyn's commercial downtown. Fulton himself is buried at Trinity Church, just several blocks from Manhattan's own Fulton Street.

Fulton Street, August 12, 1915

Furman Street One of Kings County's earliest judges, William Furman (1765–1832) was a state legislator, an early Brooklyn village trustee, an overseer of the poor, and a close compatriot of DeWitt Clinton's. His better-known son, Gabriel Furman (1800–1854), became a municipal court judge, a state senator, and a failed Whig candidate for lieutenant governor. Gabriel was also a chronicler of Brooklyn history and in 1824 published *Notes, Geographical and Historical, Relating to the Town of Brooklyn.*

Garden Place This street refers to the site of Philip Livingston's country home garden. It represented one of two walks behind Livingston's (later Joralemon's) mansion.

Grace Court/Grace Court Alley Richard Upjohn's 1847 Gothic Revival Grace Church on Hicks Street and Grace Court is the source of the street name. Upjohn had recently completed Trinity Church in Manhattan and was to embark on another (Episcopal) Grace Church, this time in Newark, New Jersey. A number of Brooklyn's leading families including the Pierreponts, Middaghs, and Packers, helped in the church's establishment.

Harry Chapin Playground (Columbia Heights and Middagh Street) Brooklyn Heights–raised musician and political activist Harry Chapin (1942–1981) is best remembered for his FM rock staple "Cats in the Cradle" and the narrative-driven compositions "Taxi" and "Sequel." He was known to perform as many as 250 concerts per year, half of them for charity. He died in an accident on the Long Island Expressway.

Henry Street Dr. Thomas W. Henry, a well-known physician and president of the Medical Society of the County of Kings in the 1830s, lived at Sands and Jay streets and was said to be the family doctor to the Middaghs.

Hicks Street In honor of their family, the street was named by the brothers John Middagh and Jacob Middagh Hicks. Their grandfather John Hicks emigrated from England in 1642, and their father, Jacob Hicks, a lumber dealer appropriately known as "Wood" Hicks, married into the Middagh clan. For many years the Hicks brothers operated the sole ferry between Brooklyn and New York. At the end of the Revolutionary War the Hicks family's land grew to cover a good portion of today's Brooklyn Heights.

High Street Purely descriptive, the street was so named because it was situated on a spot more elevated than adjacent Sands Street.

Hunts Lane Probably named for John Hunt, who purchased land from the Pierreponts in 1842.

Jay Street The first chief justice of the U.S. Supreme Court, John Jay (1745–1829) was a delegate to both the First and Second Conti-

John Jay

nental Congresses. Though skeptical at first about independence from Britain, he became a key diplomatic figure during the Revolutionary period. After the war he penned five of the *Federalist Papers*, essays that sought to gain popular support for the proposed constitution. Washington nominated Jay to his Supreme Court position, where he remained from 1789 to 1795, helping establish the court's initial rules and procedures. Jay also drafted New York's constitution and became a two-term governor of New York after stepping down from the Court.

John Street Likely named for landowner John Jackson, as the street extended through his land.

Joralemon Street A harness and saddle maker originally from New Jersey and later Flatbush, Teunis (the Dutch form of Anthony) Joralemon (1760–1840) came to Brooklyn Heights in 1803 and acquired part of the old Livingston estate. A prominent landowner, Joralemon became an elder at the Reformed Church, which boasted a veritable who's who of Brooklyn names including Abraham Remsen, Leffert Lefferts, Peter Bergen, and Theodorus Polhemus. Joralemon became famous for bitterly opposing the opening of streets through his property, though he occasionally lost to the village commissioner: in 1834 Clinton Street, for example, was cut through Joralemon's land despite his antipathy to the street's namesake and his "big ditch" (DeWitt Clinton was responsible for the Erie Canal). Two of Joralemon's daughters married Brooklyn mayors, Samuel Smith (see chapter 3) and Thomas G. Talmadge.

Junior's Restaurant (386 Flatbush Avenue Extension/DeKalb Avenue) Established in 1950 and one of Brooklyn's hallowed eating establishments, the restaurant was named for founder Harry Rosen's (1904–1996) sons, Marvin and Walter. Fulton Street on the north side of the restaurant is now secondarily named for the cheesecake impresario.

Lawrence Street Named for Captain Charles K. Lawrence, who married Susan Duffield, daughter of Revolutionary War army surgeon John Duffield (see entry in this chapter).

Little Street Tavern owner John Little was responsible, with Captain Samuel Evans (see entry in this chapter), for establishing a ferry from the base of Little Street in Brooklyn to Walnut Street in New York.

Livingston Street Born in Albany, Philip Livingston (1716–1778) was one of New York's four signers (and the only Brooklyn signer) of the Declaration of Independence. It was at Livingston's forty-acre estate in Brooklyn Heights that George Washington and his officers made the decision to retreat from Long Island. After Livingston fled with his family to Kingston, New York, where the state capital was briefly located before moving to Poughkeepsie, British and Hessian forces occupied the estate, transforming it into a brewery and hospital. Teunis Joralemon (see entry in this chapter) later acquired part of Livingston's estate. Livingston's brother William and cousin Robert R. were also delegates to the Continental Congress and Revolutionary leaders.

Love Lane Dating from before the Revolutionary War, this lane divided the De-Bevoise and Pierrepont estates. Two older, unmarried members of the De-Bevoise family, John and Robert, adopted young Sarah, the daughter of their housekeeper. She later charmed a wealth of gentlemen callers. According to local folklore, Love Lane comes from the so-called love-lines—initials of Sarah DeBevoise and her suitors—scrawled across the fence near their home.

Main Street The street was slated to become the main commercial thoroughfare of the new Olympia village, an early waterfront settlement eventually subsumed into greater Brooklyn.

McLaughlin Park (Tillary and Jay streets) Democratic Party political boss and nineteenth-century power broker Hugh McLaughlin (1823–1904) ran Kings County as if it were his personal fiefdom. Not unlike his New York doppelganger Boss Tweed, with whom he shared a striking physical resemblance, McLaughlin distributed patronage like candy and profited from insider information and sweetheart real estate deals. Starting out as a lieutenant in Henry C. Murphy's Democratic Party organization, he rose two decades later to the helm of the Kings County machine, until Pat McCarren (see chapter 1) wrested control in 1903. It was during McLaughlin's tenure that close associate William Kingsley and mentor Murphy chartered the New York Bridge Company, which built the Brooklyn Bridge.

Middagh Street Named for the Middagh family, one of Brooklyn Heights' oldest. It is said to have been named either by the Hicks brothers for their maternal ancestors or by the Middaghs themselves—likely by John Middagh, son of Aert, for whom the street was once named.

Monroe Place Laid out in the 1830s, Monroe Place has the distinction of being Brooklyn Heights' widest block and the highest point in the area. Named for U.S. president James Monroe (1758–1831), who moved to New York City in 1830 and spent the last year of his life on Prince Street in Manhattan.

James Monroe

Montague Street Lady Mary Wortley Montagu (1689–1762), as her name was originally spelled, was an English writer, early feminist, and member of the Pierrepont family. (Her father was Evelyn Pierrepont, Duke of Kingston.) Infected with smallpox in 1715, she was left bereft of eyelashes and with facial scarring. Several years later in Constantinople, where her ambassador-husband Edward Wortley Montagu was based, Lady Montagu was captivated witnessing the role of inoculation in protecting people against smallpox. Upon returning to England in 1721, she campaigned to convince English doctors of its great benefits; her advocacy was fundamental to the acceptance of inoculation throughout Western Europe.

A well-known poet and prose writer championed for her brilliant (and often caustic) epistles, Lady Montagu had many admirers including Alexander Pope, who, it is said, sought to steal her away. "The one thing that reconciles me to the fact of being a woman," she wrote, "is the reflexion that it delivers me from the necessity of being married to one." The street was formerly named Constable Street for another member of the Pierrepont family —Anna Maria Constable Pierrepont, Hezekiah Pierrepont's wife.

Nassau Street Named for Robert Fulton's 1814 ferry *Nassau,* which made a precedent-setting crossing of the East River powered by steam.

Navy Street Named for the nearby Brooklyn Navy Yard, which for over a century and a half was the metropolitan area's center of shipbuilding and maintenance. Closed for shipbuilding business in 1966, the Navy Yard has acquired a different business orientation since, with its three-hundred-acre industrial park housing movie studios, furniture manufacturers, electronics distributors, jewelers, and ship repairers.

Orange Street (see Cranberry Street)

Pacific Street Possibly named for the Pacific Stores (warehouses) that contained lard, bacon, and flour. Adjacent to them were William Barber's Pacific Mills, where cattle feed was ground.

Packer Collegiate Institute (170 Joralemon Street) In honor of her late husband, fur merchant William S. Packer, Harriet Putnam Packer (1820–1892) donated $65,000 to the Brooklyn Female Academy and had the name changed. The school has been on Joralemon Street since 1854.

Pearl Street Named after Manhattan's Pearl Street, which derived its moniker from the abundance of oyster shells that once dotted the East River's shore.

Pierrepont Street From one of the New England colonies' esteemed families, Hezekiah Beers Pierrepont (1768–1838) was a major advocate for the residential development of Brooklyn Heights. In 1804 Pierrepont purchased the sixty-acre Benson farm, helped lay out and name streets, and by the 1820s began marketing the leafy Brooklyn section. Taking on the role of both land speculator and local politician (he was also central in helping garner Brooklyn's village charter), Pierrepont worked tirelessly to recruit the monied classes to his burgeoning elite suburb.

Hezekiah's grandfather, Yale College founder Reverend James Pierrepont, anglicized the family name to Pierpont (possibly the cause of the current pronunciation). Hezekiah returned the surname to its original spelling for his own family, though he kept "Pierpont" for business purposes. A supporter of various import/export ventures, Pierrepont advocated trade with France, where he resided during the Reign of Terror, standing witness to Robespierre's beheading. He later became an important financial backer of Robert Fulton's ferry. In addition to Brooklyn Heights, Pierrepont devoted his last years to the development of his vast land holdings in New York State, which grew to half a million acres, greatly aided by William Constable, the largest landholder in New York and, fortuitously, the father of his wife. Hezekiah's son, Henry Evelyn Pierrepont (1808–1888), was a founder of Green-Wood Cemetery and the Long Island Historical Society.

Pineapple Street (see Cranberry Street)

Plymouth Church of the Pilgrims (75 Hicks Street) Famous for being the Congregational church of Henry Ward Beecher (1813–1887), it was here that the impassioned orator preached his Free-Soil sermons condemning slavery and imploring his congregants to participate in the moral work of the Underground Railroad. Leading abolitionists and other notable figures of the day including William Lloyd Garrison, Charles Sumner, and Wendell Phillips joined Beecher to weekly standing-room-only crowds of twenty-five hundred persons.

Originally called Plymouth Church, it was founded in 1847 and damaged in a fire and rebuilt in 1849. Named for the Pilgrim settlement New Plymouth, which paved the way for the Massachusetts Bay Colony, it merged with Congregational Church of the Pilgrims in 1934 and altered its name to reflect the union. In the church's adjoining building, Hillis Hall, one can find a Plymouth Rock fragment transported from Massachusetts in 1840.

Poplar Street Originally a part of the Hicks's estate and once much longer, the street was chopped up in the 1940s in the name of progress to make way for Robert Moses's Brooklyn-Queens Expressway. It is most likely descriptively named for the poplar trees once common here.

Prince Street Most likely named for Benjamin R. Prince, lumber merchant and member of the first Board of Aldermen (Fifth Ward) after Brooklyn's incorporation as a city in 1834.

Red Hook Lane Now an irregular alley sandwiched between Livingston Street and Boerum Place, it is one of Brooklyn's oldest roads and formerly a prominent thoroughfare leading from Brooklyn to Red Hook.

Remsen Street A true Knickerbocker surname, the Remsens go back to the earliest years of Dutch settlement, when Rem Jansen Vanderbeek ("of the brook") arrived in 1642 at Fort Orange (Albany), New Netherland. Of German and Dutch nobility, Vanderbeek was a blacksmith and slaveowner. Adopting patronymically their father's name, each of his fifteen children became Remsen, or "son/daughter of Rem." Vanderbeek's marriage to Annetje Rapelye in 1642 is one of the first recorded in New Amsterdam. Remarkably, all fifteen children survived to make it to his funeral in 1681. The street opened nearly a century and a half later and was laid out and named by Hezekiah Pierrepont for Vanderbeek's descendent, Henry Remsen.

St. Ann and the Holy Trinity Church (157 Montague Street) Dating from 1784, St. Ann's congregation began in the home of Joshua and Ann Sands. Their founding role and generous financial contributions to the church led to its being named in honor of Ann Sands in 1795. The congregation's first church, erected in 1805 at Washington and Sands streets, was known to Brooklyn Episcopalians as the "mother church."

One of Brooklyn's loveliest Neogothic edifices, this church building was constructed by Minard Lefever in 1848 for the Church of the Holy Trinity, whose congregation was formed two years earlier. St. Ann's Church moved into the Montague Street building in 1969, after Holy Trinity was dissolved —though St. Ann's kept its predecessor's name in the title.

Sands Street From New England, Joshua Sands (1757–1835) was a wealthy merchant who with his brother Comfort Sands had extensive landholdings in early Brooklyn. The two purchased the confiscated estate of Tory-backer John Rapelye in state scrip (Revolutionary currency). The Sands brothers surveyed land that became the basis for the settlement of Olympia, today encompassing parts of the Navy Yard and Vinegar Hill, and they were also the progenitors of the rope-making industry in Brooklyn. Joshua Sands was a two-term Federalist representative in Congress, state senator, and, appointed by John Adams, Collector of the Port of New York. Sands Street once had the reputation for being the red-light district of Brooklyn and carried the evocative name "Hell's Half Acre."

Schermerhorn Street Early Brooklyn settlers, Peter Schermerhorn (1781–1852) and brother Abraham Schermerhorn (1783–1850) were well-known merchants in New York who inherited a 160-acre farm in Gowanus. It became their summer residence until 1835, when the house and most of the property was sold. (Green-Wood Cemetery was built on much of the Schermerhorn's former land.) Further north the brothers purchased another large piece of property, establishing a ropewalk in the area that is now Schermerhorn Street. Of their children, certainly the best known is Abraham's daughter Caroline Schermerhorn Astor, who became, after her marriage to William Astor, the *grande dame* of aristocratic society and perhaps the world's most famous socialite.

The name Schermerhorn is quintessentially Dutch and is in fact a town in North Friesland province in the Netherlands. It is pronounced "Skermer-horn"; those who say "Sher-mer-horn" mistake it for a German word.

Sidney Place Originally named Monroe Place until 1835, when it was changed to honor writer and statesman Sir Philip Sidney (1554–1586). (Today, Monroe Place is elsewhere in the neighborhood; see entry in this chapter.)

Brooklyn attorney George Wood, who called Sidney "the most chivalrous of England's nobleman," is credited with the street's naming.

With a royal pedigree—he was named for his godfather, Philip II of Spain—Sidney accomplished much in his thirty-two years. He was governor of Vlissingen in the Netherlands, published various works including "The Defence of Poesy," and served as ambassador to the German emperor and the prince of Orange. His precociousness was evident as he entered Christ Church, Oxford, at the age of fourteen. He died from a bullet wound, having been shot off his horse fighting the Spanish in the Netherlands.

Squibb Park (the Promenade between Cranberry and Middagh streets) Chemist Edward Robinson Squibb (1819–1900) in 1856 formed a pharmaceutical company on Furman Street after witnessing firsthand the poor quality of available drugs while a Brooklyn Navy Yard medical officer. Only two years later he developed the first reliable ether for anesthesia, which the Union Army employed during the Civil War. A Quaker and an idealist, Squibb sought purity in food and drugs and often refused to patent his own medicines. In 1989, E. R. Squibb & Sons merged with Bristol-Myers to become one of the largest pharmaceutical companies in the world.

Edward R. Squibb, 1890s

Tillary Street Named for Dr. James Tillary (1756–1818), a noted physician during the colonial period. Born and educated in Scotland, Tillary proved invaluable for the medical service he rendered during New York's yellow fever epidemics in 1795 and 1798.

Willow Place/Willow Street Named probably for the many kinds of willows that once graced the area, Willow Place was opened in 1842, several decades after Willow Street was laid out. Willow Place residents have sometimes called their immediate environs "Willow Town."

3 | South Brooklyn

Boerum Hill, Carroll Gardens, Cobble Hill, Gowanus, Park Slope, Prospect Park, Red Hook, Sunset Park

A map of South Brooklyn appears on the following pages.

Park Slope
(Seventh Ave.), 1978

Red Hook Pier, 2005

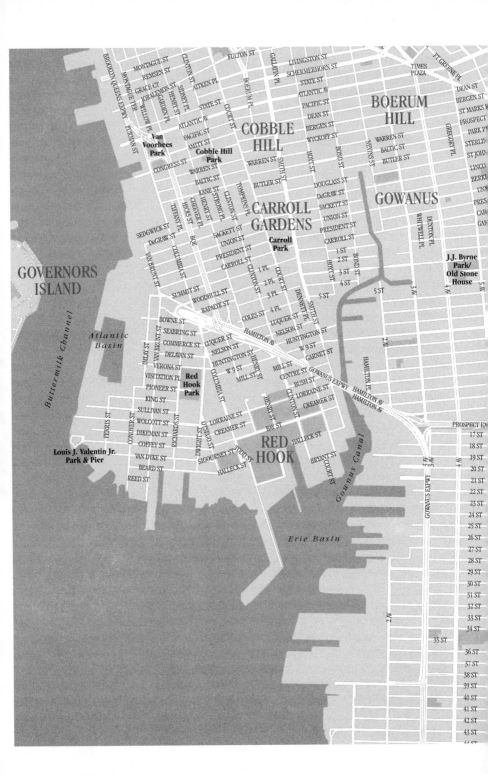

In contradistinction with Brooklyn's northern reaches (Fulton Ferry, Navy Yard, Vinegar Hill), the area covered in this chapter was mainly called South Brooklyn at a time when it did represent the southern portion of the town and city. The name is maintained predominantly by old-timers who predate the real estate makeovers of the 1960s. Today, South Brooklyn is a hybrid area that encompasses the waterfront, Prospect Park, and a slew of architecturally and historically rich residential neighborhoods.

Rural marshland for several centuries, South Brooklyn was transformed by shipping activity in Red Hook and Gowanus in the early nineteenth century, which made it a central port for the city. The Gowanus creek was likely named for the Canarsee sachem Gouwane (though some say for a Dutch word for "bay," *gouwee*). Expanded by Edwin Litchfield to a full-fledged industrial canal, the Gowanus led, with Red Hook's Atlantic Docks and Erie Basin, to increased mercantilism and development of the surrounding neighborhoods.

"Red Hook" itself comes from the Dutch *Roode Hoek,* meaning "red point." Like the origin of "Greenpoint," the name refers to the portion of the peninsula visible to sailors who navigated past. In the case of Red Hook, the point of land was covered in red clay soil. Gowanus earned the additional late-nineteenth-century sobriquet of "gashouse district" for its raucous seamen and wild groghouses.

North Gowanus, as Boerum Hill was once known, was developed in the mid-nineteenth century on land owned by the Hoyt, Nevins, Martense, and Gerritsen families. During the neighborhood's 1960s revitalization, it was officially renamed Boerum Hill after the Boerum family, in particular, Simon Boerum, who had landholdings in the area during the colonial period. A street named for him, Boerum Place, is situated on the northern end of the neighborhood.

Nearby Cobble Hill was originally called "Ponkiesbergh" or "Punkiesberg" by the early Dutch settlers and "Cobles Hill" in the initial English translation. The name refers to the once plentiful stones strewn over the area (stones previously employed as ballast for ships) and to the cobblestone incline where Court Street meets Atlantic Avenue and Pacific Street. During the Revolutionary War, the steep hill became the site of Cobble Hill Fort, where George Washington may have witnessed the defeat of his troops during the Battle of Brooklyn. The name fell into disuse in the nineteenth century, and the neighborhood, like its surrounding area, was identified as South Brooklyn. After a successful late-1950s fight to forestall a Bohack supermarket from moving in (Cobble Hill Park was established instead), newly associated homeowners sought a fresh name for their community. A realtor who had seen "Cobles Hill" on an old map suggested the name.

Originally part of Red Hook, Carroll Gardens takes its name from Charles Carroll, Declaration of Independence signer, U.S. senator, and an important advocate for the civil and political rights of Catholics. Shortly after Irish Americans settled the area in the early nineteenth century, surveyor Richard Butts laid out the streets and expansive front yards considered the "gardens" of Carroll Gardens. As young professional families proliferated in the 1960s, the name Carroll Gardens was used increasingly by both realtors and residents and became the neighborhood's official appellation.

Further east and south, Park Slope and Sunset Park are named for their centrally located greenswards. Originally called Prospect Hill, Park Slope remained farmland until the completion of Prospect Park in the 1870s. The land that became Park Slope was owned by various prominent Brooklyn families including the Polhemuses, Cortelyous, and Bensons, and much of it was developed by land speculator Edwin Litchfield, a portion of whose property the city of Brooklyn expropriated to build Prospect Park. The slope in the name is descriptive, as the neighborhood topographically declines from Prospect Park to the Gowanus. Of relatively recent vintage, the southern reaches of Park Slope have acquired the moniker "Greenwood Heights" to illustrate the area's proximity to Green-Wood Cemetery.

Sunset Park was known as Gowanus or South Brooklyn in its northern reaches and Bay Ridge to the south, adopting its current name in the mid-1960s. Only then did it take on the name of the 1890 park, which itself was named for its attractive vantage point facing west. Historically, the neighborhood's fertile soil and waterfront location stimulated some of the earliest Dutch development in the area.

Ansonia Court Apartments (420 12th Street between Seventh and Eighth avenues) Originally a factory for the Ansonia Clock Company, the largest clock-producing company in the world, the apartments are named for Anson Greene Phelps (1781–1853), a major metal-importing industrialist and (late in life) clock manufacturer. The factory was sold in 1926 and converted to apartments in 1982.

Baltic Street Named for the nineteenth-century waterfront Baltic stores (warehouses) that extended as far back as Columbia Street and onto Baltic Street itself. The Baltic warehouses stored sugar, salt, rags, and wool.

Beard Street The father-son Beards were perhaps the most significant public-works builders in nineteenth-century Brooklyn. Irish immigrant William Beard (1806–1886), a prominent railroad contractor, came to the United States at the age of nineteen to work on several railroad lines before turning his attention to building up Brooklyn's waterfront. By asking shipowners for fifty cents a cubic yard to discard the rocks they carried as ballast, and with a million square feet of sunken marshland, Beard ingeniously (and inexpensively) created Erie Basin, a massive harbor and storage depot and the southern terminus of the Erie Canal. The 1869 namesake Beard Street Warehouse (originally the W. Beard and Robinson Stores—Jeremiah and George Robinson were two partners) is today one of New York harbor's scant few remaining warehouse piers.

Trolley tracks at Beard Street, Red Hook, 2002

Beard's son, Colonel William (Billy) H. Beard (1839–1893), "one of the wealthiest and best-known men in Brooklyn," according to the *New York Times,* worked with his father on the Erie Basin and other warehouse projects before the partnership ended in 1869. Unlike his father, Billy Beard was intimately involved in local and national politics in support of Republican candidates and against the Tammany machine.

Bergen Street The early Dutch Bergen family is one of Kings County's most prominent clans. Progenitor Hans Hansen Bergen (ca. 1600–1654), a ship's carpenter from Bergen, Norway (hence the name), arrived in New Amsterdam in 1633. His wife, Sarah Rapelye (1625–1685), daughter of settler Joris Jansen Rapelye (see entry in this chapter), who came on the first Dutch ship to New Amsterdam in 1624, liked to call herself the "first-born Christian daughter of New Netherland" because she was considered to be the first European born in the new territory.

The area's most prominent Bergen descendents include the large land-holder Teunis Garret Bergen (1806–1881), who grew up, like his six generations of Kings County ancestors, speaking Dutch. Bergen later served as New Utrecht town supervisor and Democratic congressman from the Second District. Unlike his contemporary John Lott (see chapter 5), Bergen was resistant to both the industrialization of Brooklyn and its annexation to New York. He observed, "We are between two fires. Brooklyn tries to devour us, and New York tries to swallow us." His second cousin, John Teunis Bergen (1786–1855), in 1829 bought the *Long Island Patriot* newspaper which became the *Brooklyn Advocate* and later the *Brooklyn Daily Eagle*. Like his cousin, he was a one-term representative in the U.S. Congress.

Berkeley Place Irish-born philosopher, theologian, and Anglican minister George (Bishop) Berkeley (1685–1753) was one of the eighteenth century's leading British empiricists and is best remembered for his classic formulation *esse is percipi*, "to be is to be perceived." In addition to philosophy, Berkeley wrote on subjects including mathematics, Newtonian mechanics, economics, and medicine. Until 1881, all of Berkeley Place had been named Sackett Street (which is still in existence west of Fifth Avenue), but the rising cachet of the area led resident G. W. Reed to petition for something more refined. He argued that "Berkeley seemed to sound well to those who desire the change." The City of Berkeley, California, also carries the philosopher-theologian's name, and as with Berkeley Place, the pronunciation has been Americanized (Bishop Berkeley's name is pronounced "Barkley").

Bishop Ford High School (500 19th Street) Born in Brooklyn, Maryknoll Bishop Francis Xavier Ford (1892–1952) went to China in 1918 as a missionary priest and later rose to become bishop of the Meihsien diocese in Kwangtung Province. Accused with four nuns of being an enemy of the state, he spent his last months in China a tortured prisoner. Never brought to trial, Bishop Ford died in prison, and the school was dedicated in his honor a decade later.

Bishop Francis Xavier Ford

Boerum Place A farmer, miller, and political leader, Simon Boerum (1724–1775) was a great-grandson of Willem Jacobse Van Boerum, who arrived in New Amsterdam in 1649. It is speculated that the "Van" was dropped sometime around the turn of the eighteenth century to ease tensions with the new British rulers, who had Dutch residents anglicize their names. Boerum was appointed Kings County Clerk in 1750 by George Clinton and was a delegate to the Continental Congress in 1774–75. Were he to have lived he would likely have been a signer of the Declaration of Independence. Boerum was also a large landholder and slaveowner and left his nephew several slaves in his will.

Border Avenue Formerly Martense Lane, this avenue received its literal moniker when the city took title to the street. At the time, the street served as a boundary separating Brooklyn from New Utrecht.

Bowne Street Probably named for the Bowne brothers, Rodman (1784–1845) and Samuel (ca. 1791–1845), who became rich from the ferry trade, leasing the Catherine Street Ferry beginning in 1811. The brothers may be descendents of the great Flushing Quaker freedom-fighter John Bowne.

Brooklyn Botanic Garden (1000 Washington Avenue) Unlike the New York Botanical Garden in the Bronx, Brooklyn's arboretum prefers the shorter modifier "Botanic." Historian and botanical scientist Dr. Charles Stuart Gager, Brooklyn Botanic Garden's first president in 1910, thought that the term "botanic," being the older, was the more appropriate term.

Brooklyn Botanic Garden, 2003

Bush-Clinton Playground (Bush and Clinton streets) Irrelevant to the 1992 presidential campaign but rather a tribute to the meeting of the two streets; the namesakes are a member of the local landholding Bush family and celebrated New York politician DeWitt Clinton (see chapter 4).

Bush Terminal (28th to 50th streets, Upper Bay) In a 1927 *New Yorker* profile, Irving Bush (1869–1948) is depicted as an "uneven, angry energy of a man who has been confronted all his life with the opportunity to loaf." After coming into a large inheritance following his father's sale of an oil refinery to Standard Oil, Bush indeed could have sat on his hands. Instead he developed the Bush Terminal Company in 1902, a 250-acre waterfront industrial park, and served as its president for nearly half a century. The company coordinated maritime, industrial, and commercial transportation services, and the terminal, which had a railroad system, steam and power plants, warehouses, and piers, was described as "a city within itself." Beyond the terminal, Bush was instrumental in designing the nearby Brooklyn Army Base and held various high-ranking positions for the Port of New York.

Buttermilk Channel Different theories exist as to the naming of this quarter-mile strait located at the northwest corner of Red Hook and separating Brooklyn from Governor's Island. Some point to the practice of Dutch women carrying milk and buttermilk over the channel's bridge to sell in Governor's Island markets; others attribute the name to the rough waters between Red Hook and Governor's Island, which churned the milk in boats sailing from Bay Ridge dairy farms.

Calder Place Republican William Musgrave Calder (1869–1945) represented New York both in the House of Representatives and the Senate. Born in Brooklyn, Calder studied carpentry in evening courses at Cooper Institute in Manhattan and later became building commissioner for Brooklyn. He is credited with building over thirty-five hundred homes and developing parts of South Brooklyn, Flatbush, and Sheepshead Bay. In his one term as senator (1917–23), Calder sponsored the first daylight-savings law.

Senator William Musgrave Calder (right) speaking with Warren G. Harding, June 1920, en route to the Republican National Convention

---

Carroll Street

Born to an affluent Annapolis Catholic family, Charles Carroll (1737–1832) was an early advocate for the rights of colonists against the impositions of the British crown. Dispatched to Canada by the Continental Congress in February 1776 to secure Canadian support for the war, he returned to play a galvanizing role in pushing Maryland toward revolution (it had been wavering), and he eventually became one of Maryland's signers—and the only Catholic signer—of the Declaration of Independence.

During the American Revolution, Carroll used his largesse to help feed and clothe American soldiers and was instrumental in ensuring that George Washington not be ousted as commander in chief. After the war, Carroll became Maryland's first attorney general, a representative in the first U.S. Congress, a Maryland state

Charles Carroll

senator for over a decade, and a U.S. senator. He ultimately ended his political career to tend full-time his eighty-thousand-acre estate. His final official public act was laying the foundation stone of the Baltimore & Ohio Railroad on July 4, 1828.

Carroll became a powerful advocate for the full civil and political rights of Catholics in the United States. He was motivated by the persecution of his own family amid the anti-Catholic sentiment that permeated seventeenth-century English society. When he died in 1832 at the age of ninety-five, he was the final surviving signer of the Declaration of Independence. (Daniel Webster referred to him as the "venerable old relic.") The naming of Carroll Street and Carroll Gardens was likely influenced by the many Irish Americans who settled in the area, as well as Carroll's association with the heroic Marylanders who defended the Old Stone House (see entry in this chapter).

Cheever Place Samuel Cheever (1787–1874) was one of three commissioners in 1836 assigned to lay out the streets of the new City of Brooklyn. A lawyer and judge in Saratoga County, Cheever was closely tied to the Democratic Party and was a president of the State Agricultural Society.

Coffey Park/Coffey Street Formerly Partition Street, the street (and nearby park) were named for Michael Joseph Coffey (1839–1907), a district leader of the Twelfth Ward in Red Hook who rose to become both alderman and state senator. After thirty-nine years as a public servant, the area he represented was dubbed "Coffeyville," a testament to his wide-ranging influence. Coffey was one of the very few willing to take on Kings County Democratic Party boss Hugh McLaughlin (see chapter 1). That bravery eventually cost him his seat in 1900.

Coles Street Named for the prominent property owner and common schools commissioner Jordan Coles, who controlled several tide mills in the area.

Conover Street Named for John Conover, an eighteenth-century Brooklyn landowner. Conover is likely a corruption from "Cowenhoven" (itself from the Dutch *Kouwenhoven*), the name of a well-known early family.

Creamer Street Prominent physician Joseph M. Creamer (1852–1900) was appointed the first police surgeon in Brooklyn and elected coroner of the Eastern District in 1892. His son Joseph, team doctor for baseball's New York Giants, tried to bribe an umpire in 1908 and was promptly banished for life.

Dean Street Connecticut farmer Silas Deane (1737–1789) was an early participant in the Continental Congress and, with Benjamin Franklin and Virginia planter Arthur Lee, an envoy to France to enlist support for the revolutionaries. Deane's efforts proved fruitful in recruiting Lafayette and Steuben to the American

Silas Deane

cause (see chapter 4), and he was one of the architects of the 1778 treaty with France that ensured that French ports stayed open to American warships. Yet after such high-water marks, Deane's reputation and livelihood took a steep downturn. Fellow emissary Arthur Lee accused Deane of profiting from French arms sales to America, causing Congress to recall him from his diplomatic post. His disgrace was compounded in 1781 with the publication of his private letters suggesting America reconcile with England. Labeled a traitor, he went into European exile and died penniless aboard a ship venturing back to America for his first visit after his downfall. Never found guilty, Deane was formally exonerated by Congress in 1842 with a cash settlement to his heirs.

DeGraw Street Named for eighteenth-century Brooklyn landowner James De-Graw.

Delavan Street In 1839 local resident and landowner Delavan Richards purchased land near the site of this street from Daniel Richards (see entry in this chapter), for whom the intersecting Richards Street is named.

Denton Place Named for Nehemiah Denton's 1709 Gowanus Mill, an early tidal mill in the area. Denton's Mill stood on the east side of today's 1st Street, between Second and Third avenues.

Dikeman Street The Dikeman family was one of the earliest families to settle in the Red Hook area, and Judge John Dikeman is likely the person for whom the street is named. County court judge and author of the 1870 manuscript *The Brooklyn Compendium,* Dikeman (1794–1879) was for a time the oldest surviving member of the Kings County bar and, according to the *Brooklyn Daily Eagle,* "one of the few men who connected the Brooklyn of the present with the Brooklyn of the past." Dikeman betrothed Susan Remsen of the well-known Remsen family.

Dr. Ronald McNair Park (Eastern Parkway and Washington Avenue) South Carolina–raised astronaut and physicist Ronald McNair (1950–1986) died in the 1986 *Challenger* disaster. Formerly Guider Park, it was renamed in his honor that same year.

Fort Defiance Community Garden (between Coffey Street and the Pier) This green space is named for a Revolutionary War fort once located nearby at today's Beard and Dwight streets. During the Battle of Brooklyn, Revolutionary soldiers stationed at the fort fired on Admiral Howe's oncoming fleet of ships, forcing the armada to turn back and sparing Washington's troops. Fort Defiance, however, was a casualty of the battle.

Garfield Place The name was changed from Macomb Place in 1883 to honor assassinated twentieth president James Garfield (1830–1881). Garfield's death resulted from an internal hemorrhage caused by a bullet shot by Charles Guiteau, who had expected, but did not receive, an ambassadorial appointment to France. While Garfield held on for two and a half months with a bullet lodged in his chest, inventor Alexander Graham Bell attempted unsuccessfully to locate the bullet in his body with a hastily constructed electromagnetic device.

Green-Wood Cemetery Established in 1838, Green-Wood Cemetery is one of the first rural cemeteries in the United States and holds over 550,000 interees including a galaxy of notables like Charles Ebbets, Samuel F. B. Morse, Boss Tweed, Leonard Bernstein, DeWitt Clinton, George Tilyou, Lola Montez, Susan McKinney, and Horace Greeley. According to the New York legislature, a bucolic name was necessary to reflect "a scene of rural quiet, and beauty . . . leafiness, and verdure." The name came about after others were rejected, "Necropolis" included. "Cemetery" was a new term of art in the 1830s, quickly replacing previous designations including "burial ground" and "church yard." As for that pesky hyphen, it continues its formal use, the cemetery's management refusing to succumb to public fashion. The weekend picnics on cemetery grounds and the need for public space were the model for another landmark green venue across the water, Central Park. And it's fitting that Brooklyn's highest natural point (216.5 feet) is at Green-Wood Cemetery, empirical evidence, perhaps, of the soul's upward migration.

Green-Wood Cemetery, tombstone of Steeplechase founder George C. Tilyou, 2004

Halleck Street Named for Fitz-Greene Halleck (1790–1867), a satirical and romantic American poet who as a member of the Knickerbocker School sought to make New York City the center of a new American literary movement. He was also for a time the private secretary to John Jacob Astor. Halleck Street in the Bronx is also named for him.

Hoyt Street For real estate developer Charles Hoyt, who is credited, by laying Henry Street through Teunis Joralemon's farm, with beginning the process of land speculation in Brooklyn. With business partner Russell Nevins (see entry in this chapter) in 1834 Hoyt purchased the land around their eponymous streets. He also joined forces with other interested parties to petition the Corporation of the City of New York to commence ferry service between the Joralemon Street Dock in Brooklyn and Old Slip in Manhattan. This was a risky move at the time because it threatened some New Yorkers, who were apprehensive that Brooklyn would become attractive to real estate development.

Imlay Street Named for Hartford native William Henry Imlay (1780–1858), a major property owner in the Red Hook area and a member of the association established to build the Atlantic Docks in 1844. James S. T. Stranahan, later the godfather of Prospect Park, was also a member and eventually procured a controlling interest in the Atlantic Dock Company, becoming its president after 1851.

J. J. Byrne Park (Fifth Avenue between 3rd and 4th streets) Born to Irish immigrants, James J. Byrne (1863–1930) rose to become Brooklyn's borough president, serving from 1926 to 1930, when he died in office. Byrne was responsible for various civic improvements including the reconstruction of the famous Old Stone House (see entry in this chapter), which stands in the park's center. The Board of Aldermen named this park in his honor in 1933.

J. J. Byrne Park/Old Stone House, 2001

Kane Street Renamed Kane Street in 1928 to honor the election commissioner, alderman, and police sergeant James Kane (1839–1926), the "silent monarch of the Sixth Ward."

Kane Street Synagogue (Beit Israel–Anshei Emet) (236 Kane Street) Founded in 1856, the Conservative synagogue houses the oldest continuously functioning congregation in Brooklyn. Originally Beit Israel ("House of Israel"), it received its current name after a 1908 merger with Anshei Emet ("People of Truth"), previously on DeGraw Street. Aaron Wise, father of Steven Wise (founder of the American Jewish Congress), was an early rabbi here, and it was the site for the bar mitzvah of Aaron Copland.

Lincoln Place A number of Park Slope streets take on new names as they move eastward from Fifth Avenue in the direction of Prospect Park. The most intriguing change is the shift to Lincoln Place from DeGraw Street, a consequence of one of Brooklyn's legendary nineteenth-century cause célèbre murders.

In the late hours of March 20, 1873, at 731 DeGraw Street, Lizzie Lloyd King, better known by her alias, Kate Stoddard, shot a pistol at her lover, Charles Goodrich, penetrating his brain and killing him instantly. Goodrich, a forty-two-year-old widower, apparently had spurned Stoddard's advances and sought to terminate their relationship. She fled with his watch, pocket-book, ring, and pistol, though inexplicably returned the next day to spruce Goodrich up, putting a clean shirt on him and washing his body of blood. With similarly bizarre aplomb, Stoddard went to her job as a bonnet maker at Prentice's Hat Factory in Manhattan the day following the murder.

In a detective case that mesmerized Brooklyn, and after a series of false clues and missteps, Mary Handley, an acquaintance of Stoddard's, volunteered to help the police track Stoddard down. Handley was soon made a private detective to the chief of police, Patrick Campbell, and was eventually responsible for finding Stoddard more than three months after the murder took place. Shocking anecdotes would surface including the macabre story that Stoddard had secured in her locket remains of Goodrich's blood, of which she partook every day.

Thirty years later, Campbell spoke to the *Brooklyn Daily Standard Union* about the case and recalled how Stoddard shot Goodrich after asking him in an accusatory fashion, "So you want to discard me, eh?" Stoddard had confessed her guilt to Campbell saying "I did it! I killed him—shot him down as I would a dog. He was untrue, false; yes I killed him and I am glad of it."

According to the *New York Times*, DeGraw Street between Fifth and Sixth avenues was renamed Lincoln Place in April of 1873 (before Kate Stoddard was even captured), "on account of the unpleasant associations caused by the occurrence of the Goodrich murder in the block in question." Later on, the rest of DeGraw Street toward Prospect Park was also given the new name of Lincoln Place.

The murderess (as women killers were then known) was kept in Brooklyn's Raymond Street Jail, known to many as Brooklyn's Bastille. In 1874, one year after the murder, Kate Stoddard was committed for the rest of her days to the State Lunatic Asylum in Auburn, New York, a product of the new Lunacy Law passed by the state (it was actually the first mental hospital in New York and one of the first in the country). Those wishing to visit the asylum today will see the 1843 Greek Revival structure housing the Utica State Hospital.

Luquer Street A corruption of "Luqueer" and pronounced like the original, the name derives from a landholding family. Father Abraham Luqueer (1739–

1823) and son Nicholas (d. 1864), the latter a wealthy miller whose mill stood at Hicks and Huntington streets, controlled (with the brothers Van Dyke) a good parcel of the former Twelfth Ward.

Montauk Club (25 Eighth Avenue) One of Brooklyn's premier social clubs, its name was decided at a gentlemen's gathering in March 1889 at 375 Flatbush Avenue, during which several possibilities were voted on including Beecher, Constellation, Arlington, and Prospect Park. Finally, in a Native American runoff, Montauk defeated Seatalcot. Laying the building's cornerstone later that year, General Stewart L. Woodward remarked on the history of the once dominant Montauk Indians (the name is said to mean "fortified") of eastern Long Island and their subsequent drift into extinction. Despite its name, the building is modeled on Venice's Gothic Ca d'Oro.

Montauk Club, 2005

Montgomery Place After serving for sixteen years in England's military, General Richard Montgomery (1736–1775) came to New York in 1773 with the intention of living a quieter life. Instead he was radicalized and became a member of New York's provincial congress and one of eight new brigadier generals in the Continental Army. Montgomery replaced Philip Schuyler and took command of American troops during the Quebec Campaign in 1775, capturing Montreal, though later perishing during a snowstorm-blinded battle. Montgomery's body was moved in 1818 from Quebec to St. Paul's Church in Manhattan, where a marble memorial was erected on the eastern portico.

Nevins Street Named for Russell H. Nevins (1785–1853), an early-nineteenth-century South Brooklyn landowner and partner with Charles Hoyt (see entry in this chapter).

Old Stone House/Vechte-Cortelyou House (Fifth Avenue between 3rd and 4th streets) Originally built by Dutch settler Claes Arentson Vechte in 1699, it played a critical role in the Battle of Brooklyn. After surprising and overwhelming the American positions at Green-Wood Cemetery and Prospect Park, the British took the house and used it to fire on retreating American soldiers. The courageous American general William Alexander and his four hundred Maryland troops attacked the house multiple times and retook it twice, buying precious time for the rebel soldiers to escape from behind enemy lines to the safety of fortifications on Brooklyn Heights. Though ultimately defeated—and at a high price, 256 lives—the Marylanders' heroics saved many of Washington's men, averting an early and ignominious end to the war.

Nicholas Vechte, Claes Vechte's grandson, lived in the house during the

Revolutionary War period; it passed to the Cowenhoven family and then was sold to the Cortelyous in 1797 and purchased by Edwin Litchfield in 1850. Later in the century, the house was also used as a club house for the Brooklyn ballclub playing in nearby Washington Park that went on to become the Dodgers. Demolished in the early twentieth century to create landfill for what would become J. J. Byrne Park (see entry in this chapter), the house was reconstructed in the 1930s using many of the original stones. William Alexander "Lord Stirling" (see Sterling Place entry in this chapter) is remembered across the street at William Alexander Junior High School 51.

Park Place In 1873 the section of Baltic Street west of Fifth Avenue changed its name to resonate with Prospect Park, its new 526-acre neighbor. The use of "place" was thought to add prestige and real estate value—like neighboring Berkeley Place, Lincoln Place, and Sterling Place—following the 1873 depression and in light of the park's construction.

Polhemus Place The area's first dominie, or minister, Johannes Theodorus Polhemus (1598–1676) hailed from Bavaria. He spent seventeen years in Brazil on a Dutch mission (until the Portuguese took control), after which he came to New Amsterdam in 1654. Three of the original Dutch towns were in need of a pastor, and Polhemus ministered with a Sunday-morning sermon in Flatbush and alternating afternoon sermons in Brooklyn and Flatlands.

The street is likely named for Johannes's descendent Theodorus Polhemus. Theodorus (1719–1781) moved from Flatbush to Bushwick and built what became known as Mansion House near today's Meeker Avenue (later sold to the Wyckoff family). He had extensive landholdings including a farm in today's Park Slope.

Rapelye Street This small street in the southern part of Carroll Gardens is all that is left of one of Brooklyn's founding Walloon (and French-speaking) families. Joris Jansen Rapelye (ca. 1604–1662) came to New Amsterdam on the first ship to make the passage in 1624, spent three years in Fort Orange (Albany) before settling in New Amsterdam around Pearl Street. Rapelye later removed to Brooklyn, where he acquired additional property, tended farm, and was appointed a magistrate in 1655. Rapelye and his wife, Caterino Trico, birthed the first child (Sarah Rapelye) of European parentage in New Netherland. Variant spellings abound, including Rapalje, Rapalie, and Rapaleye. Tory descendent John Rapelye fled to England and had his lands confiscated after the Revolutionary War.

Richards Street With William Beard, Col. Daniel Richards was one of the leading port developers in South Brooklyn during the mid-nineteenth century. Some years before Beard's precedent-setting Erie Basin development, Richards oversaw the establishment of Red Hook's massive Atlantic Docks and Atlantic Basin, where he built a number of warehouses and factories and the first grain elevator in the area.

Sackett Street Samuel Sackett (1754–1822) worked in poor relief in Brooklyn and was a trustee at the sole public school in the area. His manorlike residence was the site of the first regular hospital in Brooklyn proper (until that point only temporary ones had existed), and he was one of the organizers of the Brooklyn Apprentices Library, which later became the Brooklyn Institute. His son Clarence (d. 1858), a lawyer, state assemblyman, and village trustee, was instrumental in helping secure for the City of Brooklyn its municipal charter and served as alderman to the new city from the Seventh Ward.

St. John's Place Formerly Douglass Street, the name was changed (east of Fifth Avenue) in honor of St. John's Episcopal Church, built there in 1885. The notorious Charles Goodrich murder on neighboring DeGraw Street (see Lincoln Place entry in this chapter) was perceived to have hindered real estate development, and the new name sought to erase the negative connotations.

St. Mary's Star of the Sea Church (467 Court Street) Established in 1855, the church received its name from the sailors who passed from the nearby harbor. Driven by a desire to increase the number of Brooklyn's faithful, the church was erected by Brooklyn-born Roman Catholic bishop David Bacon (1814–1874), pastor of Brooklyn's Church of the Assumption. In 1918, St. Mary's Star of the Sea was the site of Al Capone's wedding to Mae Coughlin.

Smith Street From Huntington, Long Island, Brooklyn's tenth mayor, Democrat Samuel Smith (1788–1872), came to Kings County to farm at the age of eighteen. He eventually acquired considerable acreage, with its core located where today's Smith and Livingston streets meet. Entering public service, Smith rose steadily in the ranks to become assessor, justice of the peace, highway commissioner, town supervisor, alderman, county judge, and, finally, mayor for an abbreviated term in 1850. By a slim margin he defeated for mayor one of Brooklyn's great public citizens, James S. T. Stranahan.

Sterling Place Born in New York and married to a daughter of Philip Livingston's, Revolutionary general and French and Indian War veteran William Alexander "Lord Stirling" (1726–1783) performed heroically in the famous Old Stone House defense (see entry in this chapter). Though taken prisoner, Stirling helped facilitate Washington's retreat; released in a swap six months later, he went on to fight at Brandywine, Monmouth, Germantown and elsewhere, with future president James Monroe, a volunteer aide-de-camp. In Stirling's postwar civilian life he became the first head of Columbia University (formerly Kings College).

Sterling Place was originally named Butler Place but was changed in 1873 by the Board of Aldermen to Stirling Place from Fifth Avenue east to honor the war hero. Somewhere along the way the "i" in Stirling turned into an "e." Bureau of Highways Chief Engineer Tillson maintained that "there is no question . . . that it should be spelled with an 'i,' although as a matter of fact the street signs all show it spelled with an 'e.' Hereafter I will see that the name is properly spelled." Despite Tillson's apparently unyielding position, the "e" seemed to hold sway, and, it seems, street signs were not changed.

The irony in the "e" versus "i" controversy is that William Alexander was not what he seemed either. Alexander fought long and hard for the right to carry forward as the sixth Earl of Stirling (of Scotland), to which he felt legally entitled after the death of his father in 1756. In the end his petition was rejected both by the House of Lords and in the British courts. Brushing aside royal rejection, he returned to the Colonies in 1761 embittered but proudly boasting the disputed title. Despite the false earldom, George Washington, ever the gentleman and likely appreciative of Alexander's efforts at the Battle of Brooklyn, used the title "Lord Stirling" when addressing him.

Strong Place Probably named for the lawyer Selah Strong, whose home and farm were located here.

Thomas J. Cuite Park (19th Street and Terrace Place) A kingpin in New York City politics, Thomas Cuite (pronounced "cute") (1913–1987) represented much of South Brooklyn as majority leader of the New York City Council for sixteen years.

Tiffany Place A former factory of the great artist, businessman, and glassmaking pioneer Louis Comfort Tiffany (1848–1933) is the source for this small street's origin. The factory, which designed the windows of the nearby Episcopalian Christ Church and Holy Family at 326 Clinton Street, was converted to condos in 1986.

Todd Square (Todd, Columbia, and Halleck streets) A working-class boy from Wilmington, Delaware, William H. Todd (1867–1932) grew to become one of the country's leading shipbuilders and philanthropists. At one time his company, the Todd Shipyards Corporation (founded in 1916 and still in existence today), was the largest in its field in the United States. He is remembered for his generous profit-sharing plans with employees. Todd died from wounds suffered from a vertigo-induced fall down a flight of stairs.

Union Street Named not, as is customarily assumed, for the Union Army (like Grand Army Plaza) but, rather, for the Union Stores, or warehouses, that lined the waterfront docks near Sedgwick, Irving, and Harrison streets, which held sugar, molasses, and other merchandise. There was a proposal in 1898 to change the street name to honor Brooklyn notable James S. T. Stranahan, but the motion failed.

Van Brunt Street The Van Brunts were an established Dutch slaveholding family in New Amsterdam, first settling in New Utrecht. Early family members included Rutgert Joesten Van Brunt and his children, Nicholas, Joost, and Cornelius. Eighteenth-century descendent Rutgert Van Brunt, a member of the New York State Assembly from Kings County in 1783–84, is the possible source of the naming here.

Van Dyke Street Matthias Van Dyke (d. 1834) and Nicholas Van Dyke (1770–1826) were major property owners in the Red Hook area and descendents of the early Dutch settler Jan Thomasse Van Dyck (ca. 1605–1673), who originally came to New Utrecht in the 1640s. With Matthias's death, the Van Dykes' holdings were sold off to the Red Hook Building Company.

Visitation Place Named for the adjacent Visitation of the Blessed Virgin Mary Church, the name was changed from Tremont Street in 1909. Bishop Loughlin dedicated the church in 1855.

Wolcott Street The youngest of fourteen children, Oliver Wolcott (1726–1797) was a signer of the Declaration of Independence, a delegate to the Continental Congress, a brigadier general, Commissioner on Indian Affairs, and, at his death, governor of Connecticut. It was in the back of Wolcott's Litchfield, Connecticut, home that the lead statue of King George III—taken by the revolutionaries from New York's Bowling Green—was melted into bullets and used by Continental soldiers against the British. Wolcott's son, Oliver Wolcott Jr. (1760–1833), succeeded Alexander Hamilton to become the second secretary of the Treasury.

Wyckoff Street Named for a major early landholding Dutch family whose progenitor, Pieter Claesen (Wyckoff) (1625–1694), arrived in Albany from Holland an illiterate indentured servant in 1637. Securing his freedom and moving to Nieuw Amersfoort (Flatlands) in 1649, Wyckoff became a town magistrate and one of Kings County's largest landholders (aided, ironically, by slave labor). After the British gained control of New Amsterdam, Claesen adopted the Wyckoff surname (*Wijk* for "small town" or "parish" and *hof* for "court" or "house"). There are sixty-three known variant spellings. (See chapter 8's Pieter Claesen Wyckoff House entry.)

Names of Prospect Park

The 1860s movement for a grand park in Brooklyn, led in large part by civic leader James S. T. Stranahan, came rapidly on the heels of the completion of New York's Central Park. The name Prospect Park was inspired by nearby Mount Prospect, at the intersection of Flatbush Avenue and (today's) Eastern Parkway. Mount Prospect was a strategic peak for Revolutionary Continental soldiers and from 1856 the site of a longstanding reservoir. Its name relates to the extraordinary vistas afforded by the mount, Brooklyn's second-highest point.

The City of Brooklyn originally intended to incorporate Mount Prospect into Prospect Park. But Calvert Vaux and Frederick Law Olmsted's 1866 blueprint, chosen for the park's design, did not include Mount Prospect in the overall plan. From the 1940s Mount Prospect has been integrated into the eight-acre Mount Prospect Park and stands adjacent to, but not a part of, the 526-acre Prospect Park.

Ambergill The name of this stream, which runs through a ravine, is derived from *amber* ("brownish hue") and *gill* ("water source").

Binnenwater Prospect Park's Binnenwater, the waterway that borders the Nethermead (see entry), was named for the Dutch word *binnen*, meaning "within." Olmsted chose this reference to indicate the area's remote quality.

Dongan Oak Monument This Prospect Park monument marks the former site of a white oak tree that New York's colonial governor Thomas Dongan (1634–1715) designated the boundary between Brooklyn and Flatbush. For years a debate raged over the dividing line; it was resolved when Dongan issued a 1685 confirmatory patent identifying the towns' borders. The monument itself refers to the events of the Battle of Brooklyn, when colonial soldiers cut down the oak tree and placed it in the road to obstruct oncoming British soldiers.

Endale Arch Olmsted named this Prospect Park arch "Enterdale" because it served as an entry to the greensward's dales and meadows. To his great ire the name was hacked to "Endale" by the time of the park's completion. The arch was one of the first permanent structures in the park.

Friends' Cemetery A fifteen-acre burial ground named for the Religious Society of Friends (Quakers). Although it does not have Green-Wood Cemetery's litany of notables, this Prospect Park resting place does house the remains of Montgomery Clift. The cemetery predates Prospect Park by seventeen years.

Grand Army Plaza This prepossessing entrance to Prospect Park takes its name

Prospect Park, 1970s

from the Civil War's Union Army. It was originally designated "Prospect Park Plaza" in 1866 and informally shortened to "the Plaza." The name officially changed to its present one only in 1926. John Duncan's monumental Quadriga-capped Soldiers' and Sailors' Memorial Arch, dedicated to Union troops, must have had some symbolic influence on the renaming. Completed in 1892, none other than William Tecumseh Sherman laid the cornerstone. The other great Grand Army Plaza in New York—better known as "the Plaza," as Brooklyn's once was—stands at 59th Street and Fifth Avenue in Manhattan and has a heroic statue of Sherman himself.

Kate Wollman Rink Funds for this 28,000-square-foot skating rink, opened in 1961, came from New York philanthropist Kate Wollman in honor of her family. Opening day had Olympic champion Dick Button on hand for a skating exhibition.

Lefferts Homestead Originally located at Flatbush Avenue and Maple Street, this Dutch farmhouse built between 1777 and 1783 was occupied by four generations of Kings County's largest slaveholding family, the Lefferts. Wealthy landholder Peter Lefferts (1753–1791), a delegate to the 1788 New York State constitutional convention, rebuilt the family's house, which colonial soldiers burned down during the Revolutionary War to drive away the British. In 1918 it was sold to the city and moved to its present location in Prospect Park; since 1993 it has been open to the public as a museum.

Litchfield Villa Located on what was the Cortelyou estate, this mansion was finished in 1857. Edwin Litchfield—land speculator, railroad developer, and brother of Electus Litchfield, who planned Borough Park—purchased the land and commissioned his residence. Built for $150,000, it was originally

Litchfield Villa, 2005

called Grace Hill, named for Litchfield's wife Grace Hill Hubbard. The advent of Prospect Park put Litchfield in a compromised position: he was forced to give up twenty-four acres of land for the park's development and sell his estate to the city in 1868. But the Litchfields remained in Grace Hill until the early 1880s, leasing the residence from the city for $2,500 a year. A landmarked building, the Litchfield Villa has been since 1890 the borough headquarters of the Parks Department.

Lookout Hill At 170 feet, it is the park's highest point and a choice spot for looking yonder.

Nethermead and Nethermead Arches The Nethermead's triple arches are situated in nearly the exact center of the park. Translated literally as "lower meadow," the densely wooded Nethermead lies directly below the arches.

Peristyle A peristyle is a courtyard with a covered walkway surrounded by supporting columns (in Greek *peri* means "around"; *style*, "column"). This 1903 Stanford White design is sometimes called the "Grecian Shelter" or the "Croquet Shelter."

Vale of Cashmere A heavily wooded area in Prospect Park, it is named after the exotic destination in Thomas Moore's 1817 epic poem *Lalla Rookh*. Moore's Orientalist work narrates the Delhi-to-Kashmir (i.e., Cashmere) trip of Princess Lalla Rookh, who meets and marries the King of Bucharia. "Who has not heard of the vale of Cashmere / With its roses the brightest that earth ever gave / Its temples, and grottos, and fountains as clear / As the love-lighted eyes that hang over their wave." A statue of Thomas Moore graces Prospect Park's Concert Grove and was completed in 1879 for the centennial of his birth.

Willink Entrance This entrance to Prospect Park, positioned at the intersection of Flatbush and Ocean avenues and Empire Boulevard, was once considered the park's back door but has become one of its most employed entryways. During Prospect Park's development, a portion of the 1835 Willink family estate on Ocean Avenue was purchased by the city.

Bedford-Stuyvesant, Clinton Hill, Crown Heights, Fort Greene, Prospect Heights

A map of North-Central Brooklyn appears on the following pages.

North-Central Brooklyn carries a cross-section of some of the borough's landmark names—Ebbets, Pratt, Lafayette, and Clinton—and encompasses a range of historically significant sites including Fort Greene's Revolutionary battlefields, the former homeland of the Brooklyn Dodgers, and the early free-black settlement of Weeksville. For the last century it has been one of the most ethnically and racially diverse regions of the metropolis.

Identified for a time as "Eastern Brooklyn" and located on one of the highest points in Kings County, much of today's Fort Greene and Clinton Hill made up the elite section informally known as "The Hill." Also nicknamed Brooklyn's "Gold Coast" for its large villas and leafy boulevards, the area was once populated by a number of Brooklyn's prominent captains of industry. (Many of the neighborhood's affluent residents believed the altitude could lead to better health.) New York senator, governor, and Erie Canal sponsor DeWitt Clinton is the source for the name of the area and of its main drag, Clinton Avenue, on which the large homes of oil baron Charles Pratt and his offspring were built.

West of Clinton Hill, Fort Greene takes its name from Revolutionary War general and military strategist extraordinaire, Rhode Island native Nathanael Greene. Greene oversaw the construction of Fort Putnam (later the site of Fort Greene), which played a principal part in the Battle of Brooklyn, helping secure Washington's retreat across the East River. Early inhabitants of Fort Greene included many African American shipyard workers employed at the nearby Navy Yard; by the 1870s half of Brooklyn's black population lived in the immediate environs. With the influx of the monied classes, Italianate homes began to dot the newly laid out streets with north-south thoroughfares boasting London-derived names (e.g.,

Cumberland and Adelphi) and east-west avenues spotlighting Revolutionary War heroes (e.g., DeKalb and Pulaski).

Fort Greene's and Clinton Hill's neighbor to the east is a product of two historic communities: Bedford and Stuyvesant Heights, blessed with some of the finest residential architecture in the city. Settled by the Dutch West India Company in the 1630s, the origin of Bedford's name remains contested. Most root it in the English, either for the Duke of Bedford or England's Bedfordshire; others, notably local historian Eugene Armbruster, attribute it to the Dutch word *Bestevaar,* or "the place where old men meet," itself a translation of an Algonquin word meaning "council place."

East of Bedford stood the nineteenth-century neighborhood of Stuyvesant Heights, named for New Amsterdam's last governor general Peter Stuyvesant. Only by the 1930s were the two neighborhoods linked together nomenclaturally. Many claim that the *Brooklyn Daily Eagle* first coined the term, but it has also been attributed to both the Brooklyn Edison Company, who did a survey of the area, and the New York State Temporary Commission on the Condition of the Urban Colored Population.

Historic Weeksville, which abuts Bedford-Stuyvesant, was founded in 1838 by James Weeks, a local African American landowner. Developed from a large section of the Lefferts family estate, Weeksville served as a haven for free blacks from the South and other parts of the country. In 1863 the Weeksville community was a refuge for black residents from Manhattan escaping the violent draft riots. Four of Weeksville's original farmhouses stand today.

Some of the African Americans to first purchase land in Weeksville were former slaves from Crown Heights. Originally known as "Crow Hill," likely referring to the crows that roosted on the area's highest hill, the name was also used as a racial epithet to refer to the blacks living there. Crown Heights took on its new moniker in 1916, when Crown Street extended through the area.

Adelphi Street Adelphi Street takes its name from London's Adelphi Terrace (1768–74; destroyed 1936–38), a town-planning scheme designed by the brothers Robert and James Adam, the United Kingdom's great late-eighteenth-century architects. The Greek name *Adelphi* translates as "brothers" or "brotherhood."

Alhambra Apartments (500–518 Nostrand Avenue) *Alhambra* derives from an Arabic root meaning "red" or "crimson castle," an apt description for this monumental Romanesque and Queen Anne Revival admixture of red brownstone, terra cotta, brick, and red tile. Formerly a luxury residence, the 1889–90 landmarked apartment block designed by Brooklyn architect Montrose W. Morris was once, according to architectural historian Christopher Gray, "Brooklyn's Dakota."

Bainbridge Street At age twenty-six Commodore William Bainbridge (1774–1833) had already received the navy's highest rank and become a national hero for his capture of the British vessel *Java* during the War of 1812. But he was no stranger to failure, having his own ship captured three times and taken prisoner for two years during the Tripoli campaign in 1803–4.

Benjamin Banneker Academy (77 Clinton Avenue) A descendent of slaves, Benjamin Banneker (1731–1806) was an important inventor, astronomer, and mathematician who at the age of thirty built the first wooden clock in America. Three decades later, on Thomas Jefferson's recommendation, George Washington asked Banneker to join a team surveying and laying out what would become Washington, D.C. When principal designer Pierre L'Enfant was fired and spitefully absconded to France with the plans, Banneker was able to reproduce them from memory and save the project. He is perhaps best known for his farmers' almanacs, published between 1792 and 1797. Benjamin Banneker Playground and the Benjamin Banneker School (PS 256) are nearby on Kosciusko Street.

Benjamin Banneker stamps, 1979

Bridge Street African Methodist (AME) Church (277 Stuyvesant Avenue) Originally built as the African Methodist Wesleyan Episcopal Church on High Street in 1818, it is Brooklyn's first independent black church. In 1854 the congregation moved to Bridge Street and took its current name. During the congregation's tenure on Bridge Street, the basement of the church was used as a stop on the Underground Railroad. The church moved to its present location in 1938.

Brooklyn Academy of Music (30 Lafayette Avenue) From its first performance in 1861 the Brooklyn Academy of Music has been one of the area's venerable cultural institutions. Originally on Montague Street in Brooklyn Heights, it once housed the city's philharmonic; following a fire, the Academy moved to its current Lafayette Street location and reopened in the autumn of 1908. Known by the punchy abbreviation BAM, it has long been a magnet to those Manhattanites otherwise averse to crossing the river.

Brooklyn Academy of Music, 1923

Brooklyn Dodgers Part of the American Association when formed in 1884, the team had several early nicknames including the Church City Nines (Brooklyn being the City of Churches) and the Brooklyn Kings (for Kings County). There was even a stretch when the team was known as the Bridegrooms after several top players were wed in 1888. It was around the time the team joined the National League in 1890 that the Dodger name was introduced; likely referring to the trolleys that swift-footed Brooklynites would agilely dodge, the moniker Trolley Dodgers was born. Still, subsidiary nicknames persisted, including such appellations as the Robins, Superbas, Fillies, and Wonders. A conclusive shift occurred only in 1933, when the word "Dodgers" appeared on both Brooklyn's home and road jerseys. The unforgettable "Dem Bums" was coined in 1940, but it would never replace the now cast in stone Brooklyn Dodgers. That is, until 1957 when Armageddon struck.

Brower Park (Brooklyn Avenue, St. Marks Avenue, Kingston Avenue, and Park Place) Named after George V. Brower (1839–1921), general appraiser of the Port of New York and Brooklyn's parks commissioner from 1889 to 1894 and 1898 to 1901. The park, which dates from 1892, was renamed for him in 1923.

Cambridge Place The name comes from London's Cambridge Terrace, one of the exclusive terraces lining Regency Park. Cambridge Place was originally Ryerson Place for the early Dutch Ryerszen family and later Trotter Street for Jonathan Trotter, Brooklyn's second mayor from 1835 to 1836.

Carlton Avenue Named for London's Carleton House. Henry Boyle (1675–1725), who became Lord Carleton in 1714, leased land from the Crown and erected his house and gardens, which became Carlton House. It was eventually acquired by the Prince of Wales and served as the seat of government until 1820, when Buckingham Palace became the preferred locale. Carlton House was demolished in 1827 and replaced with the John Nash–designed Carlton Gardens and Carlton House Terrace.

Carver Playground (Ralph Avenue between Sumpter and Marion streets) A leading educator, agricultural chemist, and innovator George Washington Carver (1864–1943) was the first African American student and faculty member at Iowa State University. Accepting an invitation from Booker T. Washington, Carver joined the faculty of Alabama's Tuskegee Institute, where he specialized in sustainable agriculture and alternative crop farming. Carver ultimately identified over three hundred different uses for the peanut, and his research was instrumental to the South's recovery from its monocrop economy.

Chauncey Street Unlike most military heroes honored with street names in Brooklyn, Isaac Chauncey (1772–1840) actually had a connection to the County of Kings. After time spent in naval operations in China and the Mediterranean, Chauncey returned to the United States to take command over the Brooklyn Navy Yard. He remained there until the War of 1812, when he was dispatched to the Great Lakes to oversee America's naval forces. Chauncey later returned to Brooklyn to once again direct the Brooklyn Navy Yard, this time for nearly a decade. Jackie Gleason, perhaps Brooklyn's most famous resident, grew up at 328 Chauncey St.

Clara Barton High School (901 Classon Avenue) Dubbed the "Angel of the Battlefield," Clara Barton (1821–1912) established the American Red Cross in 1881 based on her relief efforts in Europe during and after the Franco-Prussian War. Considered the founder of the nursing profession, she had earlier performed courageously during the Civil War, distributing medical supplies and helping to identify undocumented soldiers. Barton became the first woman to oversee a government bureau, heading the Missing Soldiers Office from 1865 to 1868.

Clara Barton, 1902

Classon Avenue Probably from the Dutch surname Claeson, or "son of Claes" (Nicholas) and later corrupted to "Classon." A possible derivation is Pieter Claeson Wyckoff (see chapter 3), a prominent early Dutch settler from 1638.

Clermont Avenue The landmark maiden voyage of Robert Fulton's steamship *Clermont* ushered in a new age in transportation history. The *Clermont* made the 110-mile New York–to–Albany leg in a mere thirty-two hours (the return in only thirty). The steam ferry, which arrived in Brooklyn seven years later, was decisive in the sharp spike in the area's population. Fulton adopted the name *Clermont* from steamship financial backer Robert R. Livingston's Hudson River estate.

Clifton Place Robert Clifton was a vestryman at Guion Church (named for founder Alvah Guion), which later became St. George's Episcopal Church at Marcy and Gates avenues.

Clinton Avenue State legislator, senator, long-term mayor, and governor of New York, DeWitt Clinton (1769–1829) was an advocate for public education, public sanitation, poor relief and slavery's abolition. Clinton is probably best remembered for his efforts in championing the construction of the Erie Canal. Less well known is the fact that at age seventeen he delivered his Columbia College commencement speech in Latin to the U.S. Congress then seated in New York or that he participated in a duel (and survived) in Weehawken, New Jersey, the same locale where Burr murdered Hamilton two years later. Clinton was nephew to New York's first governor, George Clinton, and son to Revolutionary War general James Clinton. Clinton Street is also named for him, as is the neighborhood of Clinton Hill.

Commodore John Barry Park (Navy Street, Park Avenue, and North Elliot Place) Born in Ireland, John Barry (1745–1803) was a captain in the Continental Navy during the Revolutionary War and was the first to fly the American flag in battle. Despite his naval heroics, Barry has historically been overshadowed by John Paul Jones (see chapter 7). Yet it was Barry, not Jones, who received the title "Father of the American Navy." John Barry Boulevard in Manhattan Beach provides additional remembrance.

Cumberland Street Named for London's Cumberland Terrace, part of the London Terrace groupings that surround Regents Park, a neoclassical London development designed by John Nash. Its name comes from Ernest, Duke of Cumberland (1771–1851), fifth son of King George III. An arch-reactionary, the Duke was said to have murdered his valet, committed incest with his sister, and plotted to kill the future Queen Victoria. With these pleasantries adorning his resume, he was made King of Hanover in 1838.

David Ruggles Playground/David Ruggles School: JHS 258 (Tompkins Avenue, Halsey Street, and Macon Street) Abolitionist, businessman, book collector, and first working African American journalist, polymath David Ruggles (1810–1849) edited various publications including the early black periodical *The Mirror of Liberty*. Ruggles participated in a range of anti-slavery activities including serving as conductor on the Underground Railroad, where he developed a close relationship with Frederick Douglass, whom he sheltered.

DeKalb Avenue Baron Johan DeKalb (1721–1780) was from Alsatian German peasant stock and left his homeland to become a soldier of fortune in

France. Learning that only noblemen could become officers, he bestowed on himself the baron sobriquet. Together with Lafayette he came to America in 1777, and in the tradition of courageous Europeans attracted to the American cause fought valiantly in the Revolutionary War. DeKalb served under George Washington, wintered with him in Valley Forge, and for a time led colonist forces in the South. He was mortally wounded at the Battle of Camden, South Carolina, and died after being taken prisoner of war. It was his former comrade Lafayette, nearly a half century later in 1825, who laid the cornerstone at the monument erected for DeKalb's Camden gravesite.

Dewey Place Likely named for Admiral George Dewey (1837–1917), who served with David Farragut (see chapter 5) during the Civil War and later became celebrated for his heroics as commander of the Asiatic Squadron in Manila during the Spanish-American War.

Dr. Susan McKinney Secondary School of the Arts: IS/HS 265 (101 Park Avenue) From Weeksville, Brooklyn, the first black woman doctor in New York State and the third in the United States, Susan Smith McKinney Steward (1846–1918) was also a noted lecturer, proponent of women's and African American rights, and founder of the Memorial Hospital for Women and Children.

Downing Street Named after the London street where the British prime minister formally resides, it derives from Sir George Downing (1623–1684), member of Parliament and envoy to France and the Netherlands, whose house gave rise to the noted London thoroughfare. Downing was a nephew to Massachusetts's first governor, John Winthrop.

Eastern Parkway Imagine a networked system of radial boulevards bursting forth from Prospect Park and heading to destinations in outer Brooklyn and Queens, accompanied by promenades, planted flowers, and decorative footpaths. In the mid-nineteenth century, with planning genius Baron Haussmann as inspiration, Frederick Olmsted and Calvert Vaux, together with Brooklyn's parks commission, sought to make this urban dream a reality.

Although the larger concept never came to pass (no President Street Boulevard or Douglass Street Boulevard was created, as was initially considered), two first-rate thoroughfares did manage to emerge from the original design: Ocean Parkway (see chapter 6) and the monumental Eastern Parkway. Designed and laid out in the late 1860s—largely coterminous with Prospect Park's development—Eastern Parkway's 2.2 miles from Grand Army Plaza to Ralph Avenue on Crown Heights' western border became one of the world's earliest highways and a model of urban planning. Originally known as "the Parkway," it eventually took on its current name, a simple reflection of the easterly direction of the boulevard.

Ebbets Field/Ebbets Field Houses (55 Sullivan Place/1700–1720 Bedford Avenue between Montgomery Street and Sullivan Place)

In an ironic twist of fate, not only did the great local franchises of the New York Giants and Brooklyn Dodgers jump coasts after the 1957 season, but both locales also became sites for sprawling affordable-housing projects. The Polo Grounds were destroyed and the Polo Grounds Houses constructed, and Ebbets Field—the home of the Dodgers since 1913—was demolished and the Ebbets Field Houses built in its place.

Charles Ebbets

Ebbets Field and the Ebbets Field Houses are named for Charles Hercules Ebbets Jr. (1858–1925), less a household name than Branch Rickey and Walter O'Malley, the hero and villain of mid-twentieth-century Brooklyn Dodger lore, respectively, but a key figure in early Dodger and baseball history. Affiliated with the Brooklyn franchise his entire working life (though he never played professional ball), Ebbets began his career as a scorecard vendor and progressively ascended the ranks of the Brooklyn organization. Ebbets was always eager to acquire a piece of the club and eventually procured his own 10 percent; by 1898 he was also the team's president. When he bought out a larger share of the team and became part owner, the Dodgers were playing at the small Washington Park on Fourth Avenue and 3rd Street. Ebbets helped identify a new space and moved the team in 1913 to an area referred to as "Pig Town" and to a stadium called Ebbets Field. (He would have happily named the new ballpark Washington Park but was pushed into giving it a more personal ring.) Ebbets is credited with three key sports innovations: the rain check, the idea that teams with the worst records should be able to draft first, and the Sunday baseball game. A stickler for punctuation, he nonetheless shunned the possessive with his own stadium: Brooklyn's "Ebbets Field," he would write, not "Ebbets's Field," always believing it was Brooklyn's team.

Elliot Place (North Elliot/South Elliot) Originally from Massachusetts, Henry Elliott (b. 1831) moved to New York in 1850 and became a wealthy figure and prominent person in the field of rubber goods, notably shoes and rubber boots. He moved to Brooklyn in 1857 following his marriage to Kings County native Mary A. Whitehouse.

Emmanuel Baptist Church (279 Lafayette Avenue) This spectacular 1887 Francis Kimball–designed church takes its name from the Hebrew term meaning "God is with us." Founded as a spin-off of the Washington Avenue Baptist Church, it was Charles Pratt's local venue for worship and his money that financed it. The church was known for a time as the "Standard Oil Church."

Fort Greene Park The site that became Fort Greene Park was originally the location of Fort Putnam, which famously defended George Washington in his escape across the East River during the Battle of Brooklyn. Fort Putnam was later the site of Fort Greene, named for Revolutionary War general Nathanael Greene (see entry in this chapter), who oversaw Fort Putnam's construction. Following Brooklyn's incorporation, there was growing interest in creating a park for the area's multiplying residents. Leading park advocate Walt Whitman called for the creation of a "spot lifted . . . out from the staled city, and offering all the advantages of magnificent prospect, sea air, and a jaunt into the Country." Fort Greene was transformed into the thirty-acre Washington Park, Brooklyn's first park in 1847, its name later changed to Fort Greene Park upon Olmsted and Vaux's extraordinary redesign in the mid-1860s.

Fort Greene Park, 2004

Gates Avenue Born in England, Horatio Gates (1727–1806) served with George Washington in the French and Indian War as a member of the British Army. He later moved to Virginia with his family, where he became active in Revolutionary politics. By 1777 Gates was supreme commander in the north and orchestrated the pivotal American victory at Saratoga, which helped bring France into the war. His success was such that some contend that his followers tried to replace Washington with him. Yet miserable failure at South Carolina's Battle of Camden in 1780 led to his own replacement by Nathanael Greene (see entry in this chapter).

Horatio Gates

Grant Square (Bedford Avenue and Bergen Street) The square at this intersection with its imposing statue is for the eighteenth president, Ulysses S. Grant (1822–1885). Born Hiram Ulysses Grant, his iconic name is a product of his own choosing. After arriving at West Point, he learned that the congressman who nominated him used his middle name first and his mother's maiden name, Simpson, as his middle name. Grant opted to live with the mistake, and thus U. S. Grant was born.

Greene Avenue Revolutionary War officer and strategist par excellence Nathanael Greene (1742–1786) shares with George Washington the distinction of being the only general to serve throughout the entire conflict. Though highly effective across the north, Greene is better remembered for waging a successful war of attrition in the south. A Rhode Island native, Greene's period of military combat complicated his personal life: from a Quaker family, he was excommunicated for his willingness to do battle. He retired near Savannah on a plantation given to him by the State of Georgia. The neighborhood of Fort Greene also bears his name.

Hall Street Brooklyn's first mayor, George Hall (1795–1868), served a one-year term in 1834 following the adoption of Brooklyn's municipal charter. He was later elected for a two-year mayoral term in 1855 on a platform that championed cleaning up grogshops, observing the Sabbath, and clearing the surfeit of pigs from village streets. Henry Ward Beecher gave the rousing eulogy at Hall's widely attended funeral.

Halsey Street between Wilson and Central avenues, 1922

Halsey Street James M. Halsey was a property owner and real estate operator in the area when the street was laid in 1835. He is a possible relation of Stephen Halsey, who developed and named, in honor of John Jacob Astor, the neighborhood of Astoria in Queens.

Hancock Street The first signer of the Declaration of Independence, Massachusetts governor before, during, and after the Revolutionary War, and president of the Second Continental Congress, John Hancock (1737–1793) certainly merits the designation "founding father." Though one of the richest men in the Colonies, Hancock stood firmly behind the antiloyalists, questioning authority at every turn.

Hanson Place Dr. Samuel Hanson Fox (1793–1880), a founder of the City University of New York, was for seventeen years pastor of the First Presbyterian Church on Henry Street. His Brooklyn home, "Rusurban"—so called because it evoked the country in the town: *rus in urbe*—was at the intersection of Oxford and Fulton streets.

Herkimer Place/Herkimer Street Of German background and hailing from New York's Mohawk valley, Revolutionary War brigadier general Nicholas Herkimer (1728–1777) was ambushed and mortally wounded during the Battle of Oriskany, part of the Saratoga campaign. One of the British-allied Loyalists involved in the ambush was Herkimer's own brother, Johan Jost.

Howard Avenue Named after William Howard (1725–1777), owner of the Rising Sun Tavern at the intersection of Jamaica and Bedford turnpikes. The tavern was commonly referred to as the Howard Halfway House due to its location halfway between Brooklyn and Jamaica. It was razed in 1902 for the building of the Long Island Railroad's elevated tracks and later rebuilt at the corner of Atlantic and Alabama avenues.

Howard House, Atlantic and Alabama avenues, 1923

Hull Street Naval officer Isaac Hull (1773–1843) commandeered the warship *Constitution* ("Old Ironsides") during the War of 1812. After the warship's victory over the British frigate *Guerriere*, the British Navy's invincibility was punctured and U.S. naval power established. Oliver Wendell Holmes's tribute poem "Old Ironsides" protected the *Constitution* from later being scrapped. After the war, Hull took over the Portsmouth Naval Shipyard in New Hampshire and began work on building the largest warship in America.

Hunterfly Place/Hunterfly Road Houses (1698–1708 Bergen Street) Landmarked in 1971, the historic Hunterfly Road Houses comprise four small farmhouses dating from 1840 to 1883—the sole remnants of Weeksville, one of the country's oldest free-black settlements. Originally situated on Hunterfly Road and deriving from the Dutch *aander vleij*, or "along the meadow" (a Native American trade route that ran alongside the houses), the Hunterfly Road Houses were "rediscovered" in 1968 when James Hurley, an aerial photographer and director of the Long Island Historical Society, together with engineer and pilot Joseph Haynes, flew over Weeksville in an effort to learn more about the neighborhood. From the sky, they were able to detect an alley once part of the former Hunterfly Road, along with the four Hunterfly farmhouses.

Lafayette Avenue As a result of his patriotic exploits during the Revolutionary War, Marie Joseph Paul Yves Roche Gilbert du Motier—better known as the Marquis de Lafayette (1757–1834)—was once a revered figure in America. Coming from a line of soldiers and graduating from Versailles Military Academy, Lafayette was recruited by Silas Deane (see chapter 3) to fight the British. Bestowed with major general status upon arrival in 1777, he fought immediately in the Battle of Brandywine. ("At the first news of this quarrel, my heart was enrolled in it," he later wrote.) Back in France, Lafayette was instrumental in persuading his countrymen to aid the young Americans, and he became an active participant and moderate supporter of the French Revolution, a cause for which he suffered five years' imprisonment. In 1824–25, Lafayette made a widely celebrated return trip to America at the invitation of James Monroe, during which he visited all twenty-four states. Of this period, Walt Whitman reminisced, "it is one of the dearest of the boyish memories of the writer that he not only saw, but was touched by the hands, and taken a moment to the breast of the immortal old Frenchman." No foreign dignitary comes close to the number of place names in America dedicated to him, and an American flag is draped at his Paris gravesite. The feeling was mutual: Lafayette named his son George Washington Lafayette and his daughter Virginie.

Lewis Avenue Grandmaster of the New York Masons and son of Declaration of Independence signer Francis Lewis, Morgan Lewis (1754–1844) served in both the Revolutionary War and the War of 1812, in the former as an aide to Horatio Gates and in the latter as quartermaster general responsible for capturing Fort George. In between the conflicts he found time to become attorney general, state supreme court justice, and governor of New York for one term.

Lexington Avenue Named for the 1775 Battle of Lexington, the first battle of the Revolutionary War. On April 19 of that year, British general Thomas Gage sent seven hundred British troops to Concord, Massachusetts, to confiscate colonist-accumulated munitions. It was news of this British operation that Paul Revere trumpeted on his famous ride. En route to Concord, British soldiers were met by patriot forces at Lexington, Massachusetts, and the first shot of the American Revolution—the shot heard around the world—was fired.

Lexington Avenue El, northeast corner of Lexington and Sumner, December 11, 1950

Louis Armstrong Houses (260 Lexington Avenue) For New Orleans–raised cornet and trumpet master Louis (Daniel) Armstrong (1901–1971), one of America's greatest artists. Armstrong imbued jazz music with overwhelming virtuosity and lyricism, and his path-breaking singing helped pave a secondary career in film. Never a Brooklyn resident, he lived for many years in Corona, Queens, in a house now serving as the Louis Armstrong Museum.

MacDonough Street Naval hero Thomas MacDonough (1783–1825) is best remembered for leading the victory over the British at Lake Champlain in the War of 1812, one of the U.S. Navy's greatest triumphs. A victim of British impressment some years earlier, he is reported to have said, "If I live, I'll make England remember the day she impressed an American soldier!" He died, fittingly, at sea.

MacDougal Street Scottish-born Alexander McDougall (1731–1786) was one of the earliest colonists imprisoned for separatist advocacy, in part for distributing a handbill to the "Betrayed Inhabitants of the City." A close compatriot of George Washington's, McDougall was a British privateer turned revolutionary who became a leader of New York City's Sons of Liberty and a major general in the Continental Army. During the war, McDougall succeeded treasonous Benedict Arnold at West Point and later became the first president of the Bank of New York. Somewhere along the way McDougall's street honorific lost an "l" and added an "a."

Macon Street A staunch Jeffersonian advocate of states' rights, Nathaniel Macon (1757–1837) of North Carolina was vigorous in his resistance to the Alien and Sedition Acts, foreign entanglements, tariffs, and Alexander Hamilton. Macon's libertarianism was ideologically brandished in a nearly four-decade-long political career in the U.S. House (including a period as Speaker) and Senate.

Magnolia Grandiflora (in front of 679 Lafayette Avenue between Marcy and Tompkins) Trees do certainly grow in Brooklyn but seldom one of this variety. Commonly known as a southern magnolia, this broad-leafed, forty-foot-tall, 1885 evergreen tree is one of only two landmarked trees in New York City. Bedford-Stuyvesant community activist Hattie Carthan (1901–1984) was fundamental to its receiving "living landmark" status, a first in New York City. With its large, expressive flowers, the magnolia grandiflora is the state flower of both Mississippi and Louisiana.

Malcolm X Boulevard Malcolm X Boulevard replaced Reid Avenue in 1985, twenty years after the assassination of the civil rights icon. Reid Road traversed the property of Philip Reid, a prominent landowner who served as alderman of the Ninth Ward of Brooklyn.

Marcus Garvey Boulevard Named for Jamaican immigrant Marcus Garvey (1887–1940), who through his Universal Negro Improvement Association organized the world's largest black mass movement. With formidable oratorical skills Garvey counseled uplift—"Up you mighty race, you can accomplish what you will"—and for a time sought international black repatriation to Africa. Formerly named Sumner Avenue, for the distinguished abolitionist senator from Massachusetts, it was changed in 1987 to Marcus Garvey Avenue, then following community outcry, to the more august sounding Marcus Garvey Boulevard.

Marcy Avenue Though William Learned Marcy (1786–1857) served as governor and senator of New York, secretary of war during the Polk administration, and secretary of state under Franklin Pierce, he is best remembered as the accidental inventor of the political concept of the "spoils." Defending Martin Van Buren's use of patronage, Marcy posited, "To the victor belong the spoils of the enemy." In the political context, "spoils" have come to mean the favors that successful parties distribute to their partisans. William Marcy should not be confused with another legendary Democratic party political figure from New York, William M. (some say for Marcy) "Boss" Tweed, someone who unabashedly participated in disseminating spoils through his Tammany Hall machine.

Marion Street Dubbed by the British the "Swamp Fox" for his elusive guerilla-like tactics in the marshes of South Carolina, Brigadier General Francis

Marion (1732–1795) was a Revolutionary War hero. He was later joined by General Nathanael Greene to help deter Lord Cornwallis in the southern campaign.

McKeever Place Brooklyn contractors, the McKeever brothers, Steven W. (Judge) and Edward J., helped finance what would become Ebbets Field, the final home turf of the Brooklyn Dodgers from 1913 to 1957. Made full partners, the McKeevers joined Charlie Ebbets in buying out the remaining shares of the team. When Ebbets, who was also president of the ballclub died in 1925, Edward Mc-Keever was made acting president, but he caught a cold at Ebbets's funeral and died eleven days later. Steven McKeever, in partnership with Ebbets's executors, controlled the Dodgers after Ebbets's death but became president of the team only in 1932, a

Edward J. McKeever (far left) and wife (on McKeever's right) and Ben Shibe (on McKeever's left)

post he held for six years until his own death. That year, Cedar Place was renamed McKeever Place on what was the third-base/left-field line of the stadium. Today, McKeever Place is home to the Jackie Robinson Intermediate School 320, named for the first black player in baseball, who debuted with the Dodgers in 1947.

Medgar Evers College (1150 Carroll Street) Part of the City University of New York system and opened in 1969, Medgar Evers College honors the slain Mississippi civil rights leader, the first field secretary of the state's NAACP. Evers (1925–1963) investigated violent crimes against African Americans and advocated for James Meredith's admission to the University of Mississippi. His assassin was finally convicted, three decades after the fact, in 1994.

Montgomery Street (see Montgomery Place, chapter 3)

Mother Gaston Boulevard Renamed in 1981 to honor Rosetta "Mother" Gaston (1885–1981), a community activist who founded Heritage House. The street was originally named for Maryland Declaration of Independence signer Thomas Stone.

Myrtle Avenue The first Brooklyn street to be graded and paved, it is named descriptively for the many myrtle bushes once found in the area.

Nostrand Avenue Named for the Nostrand family, whose common ancestor, Hans Hansen Von Norstrand, arrived in Flatbush in 1638. His children took the name Van Norstrand from the Island of Norstrand (the "north shore") in today's Germany. Originally called Nostrand's Lane, the avenue was opened in 1840. Over multiple generations the name has had numerous variations. It is believed that Nostrand Avenue may have been named specifically for Gerret Noordstrandt, one of Hans Hansen's sons, who in 1677 was one of the earliest members of the Flatbush Dutch Reformed Church.

Oxford Street (North Oxford/South Oxford) Named for Oxford Street and Oxford Circus in London.

Patchen Avenue Patchen Avenue in Crown Heights and its parallel neighbor, Ralph Avenue, were named for Ralph Patchen, an important landholder during Brooklyn's development in the early nineteenth century. Patchen's farm, which comprised 150 acres (located between State and Amity Street, Court Street, and the Hudson River), was the termination point for Atlantic Avenue.

Paul Robeson High School: HS 625 (150 Albany Avenue) Living a full and uncompromising life, actor, singer, athlete, and political activist Paul Robeson (1898–1976) was one of the twentieth century's outstanding Americans. Although he graduated from Columbia Law School, Robeson ventured instead into the theater. After three hundred performances of *Othello,* he established himself as one of the major actors of the day. Robeson's stentorian bass brought him further acclaim, but his passion for social justice and anticolonialism took primacy. In the midst of Cold War hysteria Robeson's advocacy was rewarded by the revoking of his passport; he lived his remaining days in seclusion in Philadelphia.

Portland Avenue (North Portland/South Portland) Named for London's Portland Place, a street laid out in 1773 by the Scottish brothers Robert and James Adam (see Adelphi Street entry in this chapter). The name Portland derives from the House of Portland and its associated litany of dukes.

Pratt Institute (200 Willoughby Avenue) Pratt Institute was founded by rags-to-riches petroleum-industry pioneer Charles Pratt (1830–1891), who came to New York from Massachusetts at the age of twenty to begin work in the oil and paint business. Establishing the Astral Oil Works kerosene refinery in Greenpoint, Pratt went on to become vice president of Rockefeller's Standard Oil after an 1874 merger. Twelve years later, in an effort to support the vocational arts and train industrial workers amid a changing economy, he founded Pratt Institute, open to anyone regardless of race or gender.

Charles Pratt Home, 2004

Prison Ship Martyrs' Monument Built to pay tribute to those who perished on the fetid, disease-infested British prisoner ships anchored in Wallabout Bay, the monument is dedicated to one of early America's most painful episodes. Allard Lowenstein once remarked, "If Stanford White's Martyrs' Monument over the remains of 11,500 Revolutionary War dead in Fort Greene Park were located instead on a mountain in North Dakota, every schoolchild in

America would know what it looked like." The colossal freestanding Doric column—the world's largest at 145 feet—was dedicated by President William Howard Taft in 1908.

Prison Ship Martyrs' Monument, 2004

Pulaski Street Recruited in Paris to fight with rebel Americans in their struggle for independence, Polish military officer Casimir Pulaski (Kazimierz Pulaski) (1745–1779) was a logical choice, as he shared a common enemy with the colonists. (The British endorsed the partition of Poland.) Under Washington's command, Pulaski served brilliantly in the Battle of Brandywine, but he considered the cavalry an independent fighting group and recruited his own international legion including Irish, Poles, French, Americans, and deserted Hessian mercenaries. Known as the "father of the American cavalry" for his efforts, he fought to recapture Savannah, though riding into battle he was mortally wounded by cannon fire. The 1954 Pulaski Bridge joining Greenpoint and Long Island City is also named after him.

Putnam Avenue "Don't fire until you see the whites of their eyes," implored Revolutionary patriot Israel Putnam (1718–1790), one of two principal commanders at Bunker Hill. Putnam was also the general in charge (and critiqued strongly for his absence of strategy) during the ill-fated Battle of Brooklyn.

Quincy Street Descended from a line of prominent Massachusetts public officials, Josiah Quincy (1772–1864) became congressman, Boston mayor, and eventually president of Harvard College. While Boston mayor, Quincy was responsible for modernizing the city, overseeing the development of Faneuil Hall, and improving the streets and correctional system. As congressman he was on the losing side of a 117–1 vote to impeach President Thomas Jefferson.

Ralph Avenue Named for Ralph Patchen (see entry in this chapter).

Restoration Plaza (Fulton Street between Brooklyn and New York avenues) Restoration Plaza is a commercial and cultural center and one of the flagship projects of the Bedford Stuyvesant Restoration Corporation, the first community-development corporation in the country. Established in 1967 by Senators Robert Kennedy and Jacob Javits, it is located in a former milk-bottling plant.

Ryerson Street Martin and Annetje Ryerszens came to the Wallabout area in the seventeenth century from Amsterdam, Holland. Along with subsequent

Ryerson generations, they owned much of the farmland that eventually became Clinton Hill.

St. James Place Named for St. James Episcopal Church, formerly located on Lafayette Avenue and St. James Place.

Saratoga Avenue The 1777 Battle of Saratoga was a defining battle of the Revolutionary War. Fought in northern New York State, the American offensive was led by Benedict Arnold, who defeated the British and General John Burgoyne. This early battle was of decisive importance for two interrelated reasons: it raised the colonists' expectations that they could win the war, and it emboldened the French to support the colonists' efforts.

Siloam Presbyterian Church (260 Jefferson Avenue) Pronounced "silo'em," it was a famous underground locale for northward-bound slaves. The name comes from a pool in Jerusalem where water was diverted, depriving invading Assyrians during their siege of the city. Milton Galamison (1923–1988), a longstanding pastor at the church and head of Brooklyn's NAACP chapter, was at the epicenter of the struggles over educational decentralization in the late 1960s.

Somers Street Most likely named after Richard Somers (1778–1804), a naval officer in the Tripolitan War who was killed when his bomb ketch (a small ship full of bombs) exploded prematurely, killing him and an entire crew of volunteers.

Baron von Steuben

Steuben Street Baron Friedrich Wilhelm Ludolf Gerhard Augustus von Steuben (1730–1794) was a Prussian army officer turned major general in the American Revolutionary War. Persuaded in Paris by Benjamin Franklin and Silas Deane to join the American cause, Steuben arrived at Valley Forge speaking nary a word of English. His considerable directions for training soldiers in military discipline were assembled in what later became the army's standard drill manual: "Regulations for the Order and Discipline of the Troops of the United States."

Studebaker Building (1469 Bedford Avenue) Once upon a time Brooklyn had its own automobile row, which followed Bedford Avenue from Fulton Street to Empire Boulevard. Named for the former ultrachic car company, the 1920 Studebaker Building (landmarked in 2000) is one of only a handful left. (You can still see the name inscribed in terra cotta on the front façade.) No longer showcasing cars, the building now has been converted into apartments.

Sumpter Street Named for South Carolinian Thomas Sumter (1734–1832), a brigadier general during the American Revolution. Having seen his house torched by the British and with the colonists' cause at a low ebb after their loss at Charleston, Sumter formed a guerilla band that helped beat back the Tories. Dubbed the "gamecock of the revolution," Sumter went on to serve as both senator and congressman. Somewhere along the line, the Bedford-Stuyvesant street name took on the letter "p."

Thomas S. Boyland Street Bedford-Stuyvesant political underdog Thomas Boyland (1943–1982) defeated a machine candidate for State Assembly and was reelected twice before dying in office at the age of thirty-nine. Public School 73 on MacDougal Street in Brooklyn and Boyland Park in Ocean Hill are also named in his honor. The street was formerly called Hopkinson Avenue for the poet, musician, and New Jersey signer of the Declaration of Independence.

Throop Street New York State native Enos Thompson Throop (pronounced "Troop") (1784–1874) was first elected to Congress in 1814, where he lobbied for a national bank together with Henry Clay and John C. Calhoun. Later, Throop's longstanding friendship with Martin Van Buren—they first met in law school—shepherded his rise in New York State politics. When Van Buren was elected governor of New York in 1828, Throop became lieutenant governor; and upon Van Buren's resignation months later to become Andrew Jackson's secretary of state, Throop took on the governorship. A year later he was elected governor outright. During his sole two-year term, Throop welcomed Alexis de Tocqueville to his upstate farm, one of de Tocqueville's stops on his celebrated journey across the United States.

Tompkins Avenue With a varied career in public service, Daniel D. Tompkins (1774–1825) served successively as state assemblyman, member of the House of Representatives, state supreme court justice, governor of New York (1807–17), and, finally, two-term vice president under James Monroe. It was on Tompkins's watch that New York formally set a date for ending slavery. Haunted for years by the charge that he abused funds allocated for the New York militia during the War of 1812, the scandal led to Tompkins's excessive drinking and financial privation. Tompkins Square Park in Manhattan's East Village is also named for him.

Truxton Street Named for Commodore Thomas Truxton (1755–1822), an important early American naval officer and mentor to future captains Isaac Chauncey (see entry in this chapter) and Stephen Decatur (see entry in chapter 1). Five U.S. Navy warships have carried Truxton's name, not to mention a street in the Bronx.

Underhill Avenue The patriarch of the early English settler Underhills was Captain John Underhill (1597–1672), whom Edwin Burrows and Mike Wallace describe in *Gotham* as a "hard drinking, short-tempered Indian fighter renowned for his brutality in the Pequot War of 1637." He settled in New

Amsterdam around 1664. There are eleven generations of Underhill descendents interred at the Underhill Burying Ground in Oyster Bay, Long Island.

Underwood Park (Lafayette and Washington avenues) Underwood Park is the site of the former mansion of typewriter manufacturer John Thomas Underwood (1857–1937), who revolutionized the print industry by developing the first "practical visible writing machine." Underwood quickly tailored his business to international languages with a reverse carriage for Hebrew and a Chinese variant that stored hundreds of characters. Underwood's widow and daughter donated the land to the city.

Van Buren Street Named for the eighth U.S. president and the first from New York State, Martin Van Buren (1782–1862) was also the first president not of British ancestry (he was of Dutch descent). Secretary of state and vice president under Andrew Jackson, Van Buren was an early advocate of party discipline and was critical to the effective consolidation of the Democratic Party. Standing tall at five feet six inches, Van Buren was known as the "little magician" (though to his foes as "Martin Van Ruin") and was considered a dandy for his time.

Walt Whitman Houses (287 Myrtle Avenue) Poet, essayist, and journalist Walt Whitman (1819–1892) was raised in South Brooklyn and Long Island and is celebrated today for his triumphant work of American literature, *Leaves of Grass,* which pushed the limits of poetic form. Of the poems contained within, "Crossing Brooklyn Ferry," a paean to the East River traverse with its evocative and mystical trappings, stands out: "Cross from shore to shore, countless crowds of passengers! Stand up, tall masts of Mannahatta!—stand up, beautiful hills of Brooklyn!" Whitman edited three Brooklyn publications—the *Brooklyn Daily Eagle* (from which he was dismissed because of his free-soil views), the *Brooklyn Freeman,* and the *Brooklyn Daily Times*—and was a passionate advocate for what became Fort Greene Park. Though he spent his last two decades in Camden, New Jersey, his writing and public persona inextricably associate Whitman with Brooklyn.

Washington Hall Park (Washington and Hall streets) This park was named for its boundary streets: Washington Avenue, for the first U.S. president, and Hall Street, for Brooklyn's first mayor, George Hall (see entry in this chapter).

Washington Park Once one of the area's tonier addresses, Fort Greene Park's eastern border street bears the former name of Fort Greene Park (see entry in this chapter).

Willoughby Avenue Named for Samuel Willoughby, prominent landowner and dry-goods businessman in Brooklyn, who came to the United States from England at the age of nineteen and had the good fortune to betroth Margaretta Duffield, daughter to one of Brooklyn's most affluent families. Willoughby founded the Brooklyn Bank in 1832.

5 | South-Central Brooklyn

Borough Park, Ditmas Park, Flatbush, Kensington, Prospect-Lefferts Gardens, Prospect Park South, Windsor Terrace, Midwood

A map of South-Central Brooklyn appears on the following pages.

Borough Park, 1970s

Flatbush Street Corner, 1970s

Botanic Garden
Prospect Park
Prospect Lake
Parade Grounds
Lincoln Terrace Park
PROSPECT-LEFFERTS GARDENS
PROSPECT PARK SOUTH
Holy Cross Cemetery
Brooklyn College
FLATBUSH
Marine Park
EASTERN PY
UNION ST
PRESIDENT ST
CARROLL ST
CROWN ST
MONTGOMERY ST
EMPIRE BLVD
LEFFERTS AV
EAST NEW YORK AV
MAPLE ST
MIDWOOD ST
RUTLAND RD
FENIMORE ST
HAWTHORNE ST
WINTHROP ST
CLARKSON AV
LENOX RD
LINDEN BLVD
CHURCH AV
SNYDER AV
TILDEN AV
BEVERLY RD
CORTELYOU RD
CLARENDON RD
NEWKIRK AV
FOSTER AV
FARRAGUT RD
GLENWOOD RD
CAMPUS RD
AV H
AV I
AV J
AV K
AV L
AV M
AV N
AV O
AV P
AV R
AV S
AV T
AV U
AV V
QUENTIN RD
KINGS HWY
FLATBUSH AV
FLATLANDS AV
NOSTRAND AV
NEW YORK AV
BROOKLYN AV
KINGSTON AV
ALBANY AV
TROY AV
SCHENECTADY AV
UTICA AV
ROCHESTER AV
OCEAN AV
BEDFORD AV
ROGERS AV
CONEY ISLAND AV
OCEAN PKWY
RALPH AV
REMSEN AV
ROCKAWAY PY
HENDRICKSON ST
AMERSFORT PL

Flatbush was one of Kings County's six original seventeenth-century towns and for some time the largest. Geographically central, from 1683 it was the county's original seat of government. Known officially as *Midwout,* or "Middle-Woods," by the Dutch, it also carried the name *V'Lacke Bos,* "wooded plain," reflecting the abundance of land covered in heavy timber and contrasting with its neighbor to the south, Flatlands, which was flat and clear of woods. *V'Lacke Bos* was anglicized to Flatbush after the British takeover in 1664.

In 1898 Dean Alvord (1857–1941) purchased forty acres of land in Flatbush's northwest corner from the Flatbush Dutch Reformed Church and the farm of John C. Bergen, aspiring to create an ideal concept of the rus in urbe. Seeking to model the new community, Prospect Park South, on Boston's Commonwealth Avenue, Alvord deliberately selected Anglo names for the streets (Albemarle, Argyle, Buckingham, Marlborough, Rugby, Stratford, Westminster), a pose also influenced by his desire to recruit "people of intelligence and good breeding." These street names illustrate the quantum shift from anti-Anglo sentiment after the Revolutionary War to Anglophilia one century later. Prospect Park South soon became a model for other planned residential communities nearby.

Kensington, named for the western borough of London, developed coterminously with Prospect Park South at the end of the nineteenth century. But there were distinct differences in how the neighborhoods were built up: the majority of Kensington's housing—one-family Victorians, rowhouses, and six-story apartment buildings—was not constructed until the 1920s, and unlike Prospect Park South, Kensington experienced a great influx of diverse immigration.

South of Kensington lies Ditmas Park, a landmark district broadly planned—from streets to sidewalks to landscapes—by developer Lewis Pounds and architect Arlington Isham. It is named for the son of family patriarch Jan Jansen van Ditmarsum of the Duchy of Holstein, Denmark, who immigrated to Flatbush in the mid-seventeenth century.

Further west, Electus B. Litchfield, son of developer and railroad magnate Edwin C. Litchfield, established *Blythebourne* ("happy home" in Scottish) from the former farmland of the Lotts, Kouwenhovens, and Bergens. Litchfield named it after his ancestral estate in Scotland. State senator William Reynolds, an owner of the Brooklyn Bath and West End Railroad, which steamed through the area, expanded Litchfield's settlement (the name Blythebourne soon drifting into obsolescence) and is credited with coining the name Borough Park.

The terrain that became Windsor Terrace, named for Windsor, England, was farmland owned by John Vanderbilt, and it is believed that English settlers in the area provided the neighborhood with its name. Directly across the park at the northern tip of Flatbush lies Prospect-Lefferts Gardens, a residential district whose name alludes to the Lefferts Manor that lies within it—six hundred lots developed by James Lefferts in 1893 using the family's land holdings—as well as to Prospect Park and the Brooklyn Botanic Garden.

Similar to other Kings County towns, antebellum Flatbush was replete with slaveholders and their attendant street namings, the most prominent being, not coincidentally, the largest landholders: the Lotts, Vanderbilts, Martenses, and Vanderveers. Most of them manumitted their slaves only several years before New York State's 1827 abolition.

Albemarle Road/Albemarle Terrace The streets refer to London's Albemarle Road in Kensington borough, named for the Duke of Albemarle, the person chiefly responsible for Charles II's restoration in 1660. Born George Monck (1608–1670), he was granted the status of duke by the appreciative king. Previously named Ausable Avenue and Butler Street, Albemarle Road was renamed in 1904.

Amersfort Place Takes its name from one of the six original seventeenth-century settlements, Nieuw Amersfoort (later Flatlands).

Andries Hudde School/Andries Playground (Avenue L between Nostrand Avenue and East 29th Street/Nostrand Avenue and Avenue K) Dutch settler Andries Hudde (1608–1663) came to New Netherlands at the age of twenty-one and in the mid-1630s purchased with Wolphert Gerritsen van Kouwenhoven, Governor General Van Twiller, and others thirty-five hundred acres of Long Island land from the Canarsee Indians. The land was later developed into the towns of Flatbush and Flatlands.

Blythebourne Station (1200 51st Street) This post office and a nearby elementary school are the only structures that retain the name of the original settlement that became Borough Park.

Campus Road The name refers to Brooklyn College, the Kings County satellite (founded in 1930) of the City University of New York. Prominent faculty have included Allen Ginsberg, Ludwig von Mises, and John Hope Franklin.

Caton Avenue Susan Martense Caton (1777–1845) lived on the corner of what is now Flatbush and Caton avenues. Her home was situated on one end of the land belonging to her father, Joris Martense, whose namesake street is two blocks from here. One block north stands Crooke Avenue, named for Philip S. Crooke, who married Susan's daughter Margaret Caton. All in all, three generations of one family honored in a several block radius.

Corner of Caton and
Flatbush avenues, 1921

Church Avenue

The road that leads to Brooklyn's earliest church, Flatbush Dutch Reformed Church, is also the source of Flatbush's oldest street name. Standing at the intersection of Church and Flatbush avenues, the house of worship is located at Flatbush's historic town center. Construction of the original building in the 1650s was at the behest of Governor General Peter Stuyvesant, who was eager to abide by the decree of the Dutch West India Company that no other churches except those of Dutch Reform should function in New Netherland. The church was replaced with one nearby in 1699, and the current edifice, built on the second church's foundations, was finished in 1795. The first minister who served the church's congregation, from 1654 to 1676, was Johannes Theodorus Polhemus (see entry in chapter 3); before his arrival, congregants had to rely on the irregular generosity of New Amsterdam ministers willing to make the crossing. Originally called Church Lane, at the end of the nineteenth century the street name was almost changed to Sycamore Street but in the end was only tweaked to Church Avenue.

Flatbush Dutch Reformed
Church, mid-twentieth century

Clara Street Clara Street and neighboring Louisa, Tehama, and Minna streets are believed to have been named for the daughters of a real estate developer in the area. Curiously, San Francisco's SoMa, or South of Market district, presents the exact same street names in identical order, quite possibly taken from the Flatbush example.

Clarkson Avenue Flatbush's most prominent English resident, Matthew Clarkson, kept company with leading Federalists Alexander Hamilton, John Jay, and Rufus King. It was King who sought Clarkson's advice in seeking to forestall the Hamilton-Burr duel. (Clarkson felt nothing could be done.) A regent to Columbia College when it opened in 1784, Clarkson went to France and Holland to procure funds for the school. His estate was later the site of St. Paul's Church, the first house of worship to offer an alternative to longstanding Dutch Reform hegemony.

Cortelyou Road From Utrecht, the Netherlands, and of Huguenot extraction, Jacques Cortelyou (ca. 1630–1693) came to New Amsterdam in the 1650s as a private tutor to the children of Cornelis Van Werckhoven. But Van Werckhoven died during a trip home to Utrecht to recruit settlers to property acquired through a Dutch West India Company land grant, and Cortelyou took on the responsibility of managing his Flatbush real estate. A surveyor by trade (he had studied mathematics at the university in Utrecht), Cortelyou planned and plotted Van Werckhoven's landholdings and named the area Nieuw Utrecht in honor of his former employer's birthplace. He is also credited with having created the first map of the City of New York. For several centuries the Cortelyou family was a prominent landholder in different parts of Kings County including Brooklyn proper, New Utrecht, and Red Hook.

Crooke Avenue Born in Poughkeepsie, Philip Schuyler Crooke (1810–1881) arrived in Flatbush in 1838, became a practicing lawyer, and spent over two decades on Kings County's Board of Supervisors. He served for forty years with the National Guard (eventually becoming a brigadier general) and commanded its Fifth Brigade during the Civil War. Afterward Crooke became a member of the New York state legislature and a one-term Republican congressman (a former Democrat, he bolted the party like many others at the outbreak of the war). Crooke was married to Margaret Caton (see entry in this chapter).

Delamere Place (see Kenmore Place)

Ditmas Avenue Jan Jansen van Ditmarsum was patriarch of the early Dutch landholding Ditmas family, which settled in Flatbush in the mid-seventeenth century. His descendents, John Ditmas and Henry S. Ditmas, oversaw a large Flatbush farm (out of which Ditmas Park was formed) and were among those responsible for establishing the Flatbush Plank Road Company in 1853. When the American Vitagraph Company maintained a film studio in Flatbush, Ditmas Avenue was the site of a home built for the day's leading stars: Mary Pickford and Douglas Fairbanks Sr.

Dr. Wesley McDonald Holder Avenue Native Guyanan and consummate Kings County political organizer, Dr. Wesley McDonald Holder (1897–1993) was instrumental in shepherding the victories of many African American elected officials including the borough's first black judge and the legendary representative Shirley Chisholm (whose office he ran for fourteen years). After starting out with Marcus Garvey's back-to-Africa movement, Holder's first foray into the political sphere was as campaign manager for the Scottsboro Boys' chief defense counsel, Samuel Liebowitz, when he ran for district attorney.

Elmore Place (see Kenmore Place)

Empire Boulevard Originally called Malbone Street, the name was changed following the devastating 1918 Brighton Beach Line train accident, which killed more than 90 persons and injured 250 others, the worst tragedy in New York City public-transit history. The accident occurred as the nonunion motorman (a wildcat strike was ongoing) tried to wheel rapidly around Malbone Street at its intersection with Flatbush Avenue. Street signs were rapidly changed—except for a small stretch still standing (see Malbone Street entry in this chapter)—to purge the bad connotations. The new name comes from New York's imperial moniker, the Empire State. Some attribute the nickname to George Washington, who in December 1784 called New York "the seat of the Empire."

Erasmus Hall High School (911 Flatbush Avenue) Founded as Erasmus Hall Academy in 1787, it is New York State's oldest secondary school and the second-oldest in the country. A private boys school when opened (the annual fee was six pounds sterling), it had an impressive cohort of founding trustees including John Jay, Alexander Hamilton, Aaron Burr, and George Clinton. The school became coeducational in 1801 and at the nineteenth century's end was incorporated as Erasmus High School into the city's public school system. Long considered the gold standard in Brooklyn education, it graduated a diverse range of figures including Barbra Streisand, Beverly Sills, Barbara Stanwyck, and Herbert Aptheker.

The school was named in honor of the great Dutch humanist scholar Desiderius Erasmus (1466–1536), who was a central figure (with Thomas More) in bringing the Renaissance to England. Born Gerhard Gerhards, Erasmus took on a Latinized name, a practice in vogue at the time. (A statue of him stands outside the original eighteenth-century building in the main courtyard.) The school has recently been reorganized into several smaller bodies, all carrying in part the Erasmus Hall name. Adjacent Erasmus Street takes its name from the school.

Farragut Place/Farragut Road Named for one of the best-known Civil War naval commanders, David Glasgow Farragut (1801–1870), "First Admiral of the Navy" and speaker of the quotable "Damn the torpedoes, full speed ahead!" Though a southerner, he firmly backed the Union, always maintaining that was "sticking to the flag." The nearby neighborhood is still occasionally labeled Farragut. One can find heroic statues of him at Madison Square Park and in Washington, D.C., at Farragut Square.

Farrell's Bar (215 Prospect Park West at 16th Street) A legendary neighborhood bar made famous via Pete Hamill's journalism, the watering hole was opened by Mike Farrell in 1933, after Prohibition's repeal. The bar carries on a tradition of tap beer in disposable cups.

Fenimore Street Named by Margaret Bartlett, the wife of city surveyor and vice president of the Flatbush Water Company Dr. Homer L. Bartlett, for James Fenimore Cooper (1789–1851), an early American author known for his frontier adventure novels, notably *The Last of the Mohicans,* penned in 1826. Margaret's father was a friend of Fenimore Cooper's.

Fiske Terrace (bounded by Ocean Avenue, Glenwood Road, the LIRR, and the BMT) A planned suburban development administered by the T. B. Ackerson Company and named for the former Fiske estate, which stood on the site. In 1905 T. B. Ackerson paid George P. and Elizabeth Fiske $285,000 for their Flatbush property, which included a mansion (since demolished) called Fiske Terrace. The Avenue H station (now landmarked) of the Brighton Beach Line was once called the Fiske Terrace station.

Flatbush Avenue The first settlers in Flatbush lived along a Native American path that went up to Flatlands (then Nieuw Amersfoort). It was this trail that became Flatbush Avenue, named after the town of Flatbush. Originally called Flatbush Road or Main Street, it was opened from the village of Flatbush to Prospect Hill in 1854.

Foster Avenue This avenue was named for James Foster, whose family settled in Brooklyn in the eighteenth century and was also among the early settlers in Jamaica, Queens county.

Franklin Avenue Running westward from Flatbush Avenue, Franklin Avenue remembers early Quaker settler John Franklin, whose property ran alongside it. Prior to Franklin's purchase, the land had been a part of the Martense farm.

Friel Place Formerly Montgomery Street, it was renamed in 1933 in memory of George W. Friel (d. 1928), a Democratic alderman from Brooklyn's Forty-seventh District who died in office.

Harry Maze Memorial Park (Avenue D between East 56th and East 57th streets) Attorney Harry Maze (1902–1971) served Brooklyn in a variety of ways including assistant district attorney, assistant deputy comptroller, and council member from the Twenty-sixth District. He was a close political ally of longtime Brooklyn Democratic Party boss Stanley Steingut. The park was named in 1973.

Hawthorne Street Like his contemporary James Fenimore Cooper, American writer Nathaniel Hawthorne (1804–1864) is also honored by a Flatbush street name. Hawthorne wrote short stories and novels including *The Scarlet Letter* and *The House of Seven Gables.* Born in Salem, Massachusetts, he was a descendent of John Hawthorne, a residing magistrate at the Salem witch trials.

Hillel Place The street takes its name from the 1959 Brooklyn College Hillel Building. The first-century Jerusalem philosopher Hillel formulated basic interpretations of rabbinic law and became head of the *Sanhedrin,* or Jewish supreme court. He is best remembered today for his contributions to ethics and famously wrote, "If I am not for myself, who will be for me? And if I am only for myself, then what am I? And if not now, when?" Hillel Place was originally called Germania Place for the Germania Land Improvement Company, which under the direction of Henry Meyer turned the area's farmland into planned communities.

Kenmore Place The names of Kenmore Place, Elmore Place, Delamere Place, and Mansfield Place were abruptly changed in the 1930s to the less dulcet-sounding East 21st, 22nd, 23rd, and 24th streets. In 2001, after fifteen years of community advocacy, the English-connoting names were reinstated. Rare is the case when previous street names are restored, a practice more commonly reserved for countries wracked by revolutionary interludes.

Kings Highway Flatbush's southern flank and originally a Canarsee Indian trail, it was named in 1704 for Kings County and became the road connecting the county's earliest settlements. Some claim it to be the first designated

Kings Highway, 1970s

"highway" in the United States. In the early nineteenth century, Kings Highway was the name given to a complex of roads: the central Ferry Road, which ran from the Brooklyn Ferry through Kings County and the counties of Queens and Suffolk, and feeder roads that connected into Ferry Road from other small towns.

Lefferts Manor Named for James Lefferts of the Dutch Lefferts family, who divided a section of his northern Flatbush farm in 1893 into six hundred lots for development, Lefferts Manor is an eight-block rectangle within the neighborhood of Prospect-Lefferts Gardens and an exquisite enclave of residential architecture. Seeking to establish a stable middle-class neighborhood, Lefferts attached certain conditions to ownership: homes built on the land had to be single-family residences, built of brick or stone, at least two stories high, and recessed back from the street. In its earlier days Lefferts Manor was no model of ethnic and racial pluralism—even Jackie Robinson was rejected as a neighbor. The Lefferts Homestead (see chapter 3), which now resides in Prospect Park, was originally James Lefferts's farmhouse.

Linden Boulevard Renamed three times, it was dubbed Linden Boulevard for the abundant linden trees in the area. The boulevard has a long expanse running from central Brooklyn through Queens and into Nassau County, with its termination at the Southern State Parkway.

Lott Place/Lott Street French Huguenots from Drenten, Holland, Englebart Lott and sons arrived in New Amsterdam in 1652. (Englebart's son Pieter was the first to settle in Flatbush.) By the late eighteenth century the Lotts were one of Flatbush's largest landholding and slaveholding families. (Johannes Lott topped Kings County overall with sixteen slaves in 1790.) The Lotts were also key figures in the modernization of Flatbush, prominent lawyer John (Judge) A. Lott (1805–1878) taking a leading role. Beyond holding various legal and political offices—state assemblyman, senator, supreme court and appeals court judge—Lott was president of the Flatbush Board of Improvement and the Brooklyn, Flatbush, and Coney Island Railroad Company. No less an authority than Oliver Wendell Holmes, Sr., once called him the "ablest lawyer" in Brooklyn. Lott shared a law practice with Henry C. Murphy (see Senator Street entry in chapter 7) and Judge John Vanderbilt (see entry in this chapter), their office serving as informal headquarters for influential Democratic Party insiders.

Louisa Street (see Clara Street)

Maimonides Medical Center (Tenth Avenue and 48th Street) Known by his Greek name, Maimonides, Moshe ben Maimon (both Maimonides and "ben Maimon" translate as "son of Maimon") was an important medieval philosopher, physician, and rabbi. A Sephardic Jew from Spain, Maimonides (1135–1204) studied in Morocco, where he published his important commentary on the Mishna and penned his *Guide to the Perplexed*. He spent the remainder of his life in Egypt practicing medicine (as a court physician) and religion (as Cairo's chief rabbi). The hospital's name dates from 1947, when United Israel Zion merged with Beth Moses Hospital.

Malbone Street There is only this little sliver left from the once longer street renamed Empire Boulevard (see entry in this chapter) after the violent 1918 train wreck. Developer Ralph Malbone in the 1830s laid out the area known for a time as Malboneville.

Mansfield Place (see Kenmore Place)

Marlborough Road For Marlborough Road in England, a street near St. James Park.

Martense Court/Martense Street Influential Flatbush resident Joris Martense (1724–1791) maintained dual allegiances during the British occupation of Brooklyn: hedging his bets, Martense supported the king but also gave a significant amount of money to the patriot cause. With other distinguished citizens of Flatbush, Martense promoted the establishment of Erasmus Hall Academy (see entry in this chapter) in 1787. His grandfather Martin Adriance (1668–1754) was Flatbush's largest landholder whose three sons, following custom, took his first name for their surname.

McDonald Avenue Formerly Gravesend Avenue, it was renamed in the 1930s for John R. McDonald (d. 1932), chief clerk of the Kings County Surrogate's Court. McDonald's death was unexpected, caused by the swallowing of a piece of chicken bone puncturing his intestine. His son, Miles McDonald, was both a judge and district attorney of Kings County.

Micieli Place Opened in the 1940s, this short street was named for the real estate speculator who developed the area.

Minna Street (see Clara Street)

Newkirk Avenue Cornelissen van Nieuwkercke (born ca. 1600) of Gelderland, the Netherlands, was the father of Garret Cornelissen van Nieuwkercke, who with his brother Mattheus came to Flatbush on the Dutch ship *De Moesman* in 1659. Garret's Flatbush farm, through which Newkirk Avenue was laid, is the source of the street name. By the fourth generation, the name of the family was transformed to Newkirk; translated from the Dutch, the name means "from the New Church," likely alluding to a neighboring church in the family's original Utrecht village.

Ocean Avenue Unlike Ocean Parkway (see entry below), Ocean Avenue misses the ocean altogether, terminating at Sheepshead Bay.

Ocean Parkway Blessed by Olmsted and Vaux's expert boulevard-style design, the five-and-one-half-mile Ocean Parkway was finished in 1876 and connected Prospect Park to the resorts of Coney Island. (The name Ocean Parkway refers to the water at its southern terminus.) In 1894 it became the site of the country's first bike path.

Rugby Road Rugby Road derives from the same-named small thoroughfare in the borough of Ealing, London.

St. Paul's Court/St. Paul's Place (157 St. Paul's Place) Named for the Episcopal church, St. Paul's Church-in-the-Village of Flatbush, founded in 1837.

Sgt. Joyce Kilmer Triangle (Kings Highway, Quentin Road, and East 12th Street) Death on a 1918 French battlefield may have ended (Alfred) Joyce Kilmer's life (1886–1918), but through his poetry, in particular the well-known "Trees," not to mention the place-names here in Midwood and on the Grand Concourse in the Bronx, his name lives on. At the dedication ceremony in 1929, Kilmer's mother described her son as "one of the many whose hearts in those stirring days were stronger than their brains."

Sherman Street Senator and representative from Connecticut, Roger Sherman (1721–1793) was the only politician to sign the four seminal documents relating to America's birth: the Declaration of Colonial Rights, the Declaration of Independence, the Articles of Confederation, and the Constitution. Regarding the Constitution, Sherman was instrumental in forging the Connecticut (later Great) Compromise, which through a bicameral legislature defined equitable representation for large and small states and quantified slaves as three-fifths of a person. (Connecticut earned its "Constitution State" nickname for this.)

Sid Luckman Field (Avenue M and McDonald Parkway) Peering out from the F train between the Bay Parkway and Avenue N stops, one has a panoramic view of Erasmus High School's Sid Luckman field. A child of German-Jewish immigrants, Sid Luckman (1916–1998) was a native Brooklynite who made his name as a star quarterback for George Halas's Chicago Bears. The Hall-of-Famer revolutionized the "T formation" and was at the helm during the 1940 championship game that saw the Bears annihilate the Redskins 73–0. "No field general ever called plays more artistically," gushed the New York Times. Luckman was an Erasmus High School phenom and led the school to two city championships.

Henry Warner Slocum

Slocum Place Brooklyn lawyer Henry Warner Slocum (1827–1894) was a Civil War major general who fought at Antietam, Gettysburg, and during Sherman's famous "march to the sea." He was later a three-term congressman and served as controller of Brooklyn's Board of City Works. Alas, we are most often reminded of Slocum by mention of the catastrophic 1904 steamship disaster in which over one thousand people (mostly German immigrants) perished in the East River. The ship was called the *General Slocum.*

Snyder Avenue The avenue is named for the Snyders (Dutch for "tailor"), a landowning Dutch family in Flatbush. On the street stands the 1875 Flatbush Town Hall building that became a symbol of the town's strongly guarded independence. (Two years earlier Flatbush's citizens voted down incorporation into greater Brooklyn.) Independence would be preserved for only another nineteen years.

Tennis Court

Story Court/Story Street Named for the Dutch Story family, who owned a large swath of property in the area that is now Church and McDonald avenues.

Tehama Street (see Clara Street)

Tennis Court It was the local entrepreneur Richard Ficken that (punningly) named the street and launched the residential development of Tennis Court. Dating from 1887 it was a precursor to the suburbanized urban grids of Prospect Park South and Ditmas Park.

Samuel Tilden, 1876

Tilden Avenue Formerly Vernon Avenue, the name was changed to honor Samuel Tilden (1814–1886), established attorney and Democratic governor of New York who did battle with Boss Tweed's corrupt Tammany Ring (eventually leading to Tweed's arrest and imprisonment). However, Tilden's reform triumphs did not help him on the national scene: in the most contested presidential election of the nineteenth century, Tilden came up one electoral college vote shy to Rutherford B. Hayes despite gaining the popular vote. Along with the library collections of the Astor and Lenox families, nearly half of Tilden's sizable estate went to establishing the New York Public Library.

Vanderbilt Street Jan Aertsen Vanderbilt (ca. 1627–1704) arrived in Flatbush sometime in the mid-1650s. His quintessentially Dutch family name, Van der Bilt, is sometimes translated as "from the town of Bilt" in Utrecht. Scion John Vanderbilt, for whom the street is named, was a prominent politician and jurist in the mid-nineteenth century and husband of local historian Gertrude Lefferts Vanderbilt. Valedictorian at Columbia College, Vanderbilt became a partner at the law office of Judge John A. Lott (see entry in this chapter) and Henry C. Murphy (see chapter 7), both of whom held great political sway in Kings County. An active state senator, Vanderbilt was later nominated (in 1853) to be the Democratic candidate for New York's lieutenant governor. But his political career abruptly ended when he was forced to withdraw from public life because of poor health.

Vanderveer Place The Dutch Vanderveers, whose name translates as either "from the ferry" or "of the village of Veere," trace their new world roots to Cornelis Janszen Vanderveer (d. 1703), who immigrated to New Amsterdam in 1659 and thereafter purchased farmland in Flatbush (land that stayed in the family until 1906). Grandson Cornelis Vanderveer (ca. 1696–1782), captain of the Flatbush militia during the Revolutionary War, was captured and set to hang when a British officer whom he knew prior to the conflict interceded on his behalf. His sons, Gerret and John C. Vanderveer, kept adjoining large Flatbush farms.

The Vanderveer family home, long considered one of the best examples of Colonial Dutch architecture, was destroyed in 1912 to make way for Vanderveer Place. The locally prominent Vanderveer mill, present on the farm until 1879 when it was destroyed by fire, was used to shelter blacks during the violent 1863 Civil War draft riots. Vanderveer Park, a Flatbush subdivision, became for a time a popular late-nineteenth-century middle-class development. The 1957 Vanderveer Estates is the largest apartment complex today in East Flatbush.

Baseball Opening Day, Ebbets Field, April 2, 1914. Postmaster Kelly throws out the first ball with Ebbets looking on.

Veronica Place Sister Agnes Veronica (Stapleton) (d. 1939), principal of the Holy Cross Parish School, is the source for this Flatbush street.

William E. Kelly Memorial Park (Avenue S, East 14th Street, and East 8th Street) Named for William E. Kelly (1872–1929), head of the National Letter Carriers Association before President Wilson appointed him Kings County Postmaster in 1914. Afterward, he spent thirteen years as clerk of Kings County. Together with Mayor Jimmy Walker, who called Kelly "one of New York's finest citizens," more than ten thousand persons paid their respects at his funeral.

Wingate Park/George Wingate High School (Brooklyn Avenue, Rutland Road/ 600 Kingston Avenue) Unhappy with the marksmanship of Union soldiers, Civil War National Guardsman and Union general George Wingate (1840–1928) in 1871 cofounded with Colonel William Church the National Rifle Association (NRA). A few years after its birth, Wingate founded a system of instruction for rifle practice that was later incorporated into National Guard and U.S. Army training procedures.

Woodruff Avenue Republican leader and businessman Timothy Woodruff (1858–1913) chaired the New York Republican State Committee, was Kings County parks commissioner, and served as lieutenant governor under Teddy Roosevelt. Yet higher office eluded him—some say because of the relentless caricature about his alleged foplike sartorial excesses. When he sought the vice presidential nomination in 1900, Republican boss Mark Hanna charged that Woodruff was known only for his "fancy waistcoats." Woodruff himself later lamented, "Sometimes I think that if I had been careless in my dress, and perhaps a little unclean, as some geniuses are said to be—long nails, ragged hair . . . I might have made things easier for myself."

Wyckoff-Bennett Home, 2005

Woods Place Named for the Roman Catholic clergyman Father John T. Woods (1860–1924), pastor of the Holy Cross Roman Catholic Church from 1892 to 1924. During his tenure Woods built a new convent and rectory for the church, his accomplishments ultimately elevating him to the rank of monsignor.

Wyckoff-Bennett Homestead (1669 East 22nd Street at Kings Highway) Brooklyn's only pre-Revolutionary Dutch colonial house in privately owned hands. Henry and Abraham Wyckoff, descendents of early settler Pieter Wyckoff, were the original inhabitants when the home was built in 1766. During the Revolutionary War, Hessian soldiers were quartered in the house (extant carvings, *auf Deutsch,* are testament to the fact). Cornelius Bennett purchased Wyckoff's hundred-acre farm in 1835, and the home was occupied by Bennett family members well into the twentieth century (the last of whom being Brooklyn poet Gertrude Ryder Bennett).

6 | Eastern Brooklyn

**Brownsville, Canarsie, Cypress Hills,
East New York, New Lots**

A map of Eastern Brooklyn appears on the following pages.

Amboy Street, 1940s

L ocated at the easternmost point of the historic town of Flatbush, the district of New Lots was originally named *Ostwout*, or "East Woods," by the Dutch. It received its new appellation in the 1670s from farmers residing in Flatbush and Flatlands who moved to New Lots to live and work on previously untilled land. The name was given in contradistinction to the western part of Flatbush—Old Lots—from which many of the farmers migrated. Seldom used today, the New Lots name is usually recognized by city residents only as the last stop on the subway's No. 3 train line.

The original farming families of New Lots included the Van Sicklens, Wyckoffs, and Stoothoffs, and it was they that wealthy Connecticut merchant John Pitkin approached in 1835 to purchase land. Pitkin chose the name East New York for his nearby development, anticipating that it could become an eastern metropolitan counterpoint to New York City. With the 1837 panic, however, Pitkin's finances dried up and his best-laid plans failed to materialize. Twenty years later Pitkin's dream was partially realized when Horace Miller and James Butler purchased property east of Wyckoff Avenue, developing it into residential lots, changing the nature of the village, and attracting many new residents.

New Lots was officially separated from Flatbush and incorporated as a town in 1852, absorbing its neighboring communities—Cypress Hills, Brownsville, and East New York. The neighborhood of Cypress Hills, situated on the border of Brooklyn and Queens, was originally called Union Place after the area's popular Union Course Racetrack, built in 1821. Later renamed Cypress Hills for the cypress trees covering the local hills, its bucolic locale eventually became a burial ground for the Civil War dead.

The adjacent Brownsville neighborhood is named for Vermont native Charles S. Brown, who began investing in the western portion of New Lots in 1865, spending over a decade developing the area. Brown acquired and subdivided a significant amount of farmland from the Lott family, the Van Sinderens, and the Vanderveers and built several hundred frame cottages. The area was originally called Brown's Village, later morphed into Brownsville—and would become the site for successive waves of European immigrants.

Formerly part of the original town of Flatlands, neighboring Canarsie is named for the Canarsee Indians once resident throughout Western Long Island. The group's name derives from the Algonquin word for "fort," "fenced land," or "palisade."

Amboy Street Likely named after the New Jersey town of Perth Amboy, the name has Algonquin roots. Made famous by Irving Shulman's 1946 novel *The Amboy Dukes,* which spotlighted Jewish youth gangs and working-class alienation, this Brownsville street was also the home to Margaret Sanger's first birth-control clinic.

Arlington Avenue Named for Arlington National Cemetery in Virginia, the burial ground established around the appropriated home of Robert E. Lee in 1864.

Ashford Street Formerly Adams Street, the name was anglicized to Ashford most likely to raise the neighborhood's stature. Located in Kent, England, Ashford was a market town within the farms of the Romney Marsh.

Barbey Street Named for Andrew Barbey, a nineteenth-century landowner whose property was located near East New York Avenue and Thatford Street.

Belmont Avenue

Born August Schoenberg in Germany's Rhineland, August Belmont (1816–1890) was a rags-to-riches story. Starting out as a floor sweeper for the House of Rothschild in Frankfurt, he rose to become a Wall Street financier and marry the daughter of Commodore Matthew Perry. With Leonard Jerome (see entry in this chapter) Belmont founded the American Jockey Club and Jerome Park; he also financed the Belmont Stakes, the final horse race of the Triple Crown. Belmont, who threw lavish parties at his Manhattan Fifth Avenue home, was the model for the character Julius Beaufort in Edith Wharton's *Age of Innocence*. His son, August Belmont Jr., was the force behind New York City's first subway, the Interborough Rapid Transit (the IRT), in 1904.

August Belmont, between 1855 and 1865

Berriman Street Named for William Berriman of the *Buffalo Evening News,* a friend of New Lots Democratic Party leader Harry H. Adams (see Folsom entry in this chapter).

Betsy Head Playground (Dumont Avenue, Livonia Avenue, Strauss Street, and Thomas Boyland Street) This ten-acre recreational space honors British immigrant and property owner Betsy Head (1851–1907), who bequeathed the city $190,000 for the facilities. Head was brought from England by millionaire merchant George C. Taylor to manage his estate. She disowned her daughter for marrying one of the estate's foremen, and in her will left her only five dollars of a $365,000 fortune.

Blake Avenue Dutch farmer John Blake (1746–1828) was one of New Lots' early settlers and helped found the New Lots Reformed Church in 1823. In the 1930s and 1940s Blake Avenue was the scene of various bloody incidents involving the notorious Brooklyn mob Murder, Inc. It was here that Abraham Reles, a contract killer, murdered Brooklyn rackets boss Irving Shapiro. Reles, known as the "Terror of Brownsville," later gave testimony that eventually led to Murder, Inc.'s dissolution.

Bradford Street Publisher and printer William Bradford (1663–1752) in 1690 founded one of the first paper mills in the Colonies. Printing a pamphlet critical of Pennsylvania's Quaker government in 1692 led to his arrest and jailing and resulted in one of the earliest freedom-of-expression cases to be heard. Bradford later moved to New York and published the city's first newspaper, the *New York Gazette,* a mouthpiece for Governor William Cosby. Bradford is buried in Trinity Church in Manhattan, and his tombstone, making reference to his robust ninety-two years, says, "Reader, reflect how too you'll quit this stage: you'll find but few attain to such an age." Bradford Street had been called Butler, after Massachusetts governor Benjamin Franklin Butler, but the name was changed in 1887.

Bulwer Place A British writer and career diplomat with posts in Constantinople, Madrid, Florence, Bucharest, and Washington, Sir Henry Lytton Bulwer (1801–1872) helped negotiate the controversial Clayton-Bulwer Treaty in 1850, which sought to resolve various Anglo-American disputes in Latin America.

Cemetery of the Evergreens (1629 Bushwick Avenue) The 1849 nondenominational cemetery is likely named for the several thousand evergreen trees brought from the Catskills by Rev. John D. Wells. Prominent interees include dancer Bill "Bojangles" Robinson, morals crusader Anthony Comstock, and murdered New York City councilman James E. Davis, who was moved here after it was learned that he and his assassin shared resting places in Green-Wood Cemetery.

Cleveland Street Named after President Grover Cleveland (1837–1908), the only president to be elected for nonconsecutive terms and the only one married in the White House (he wed the twenty-one-year-old Frances Folsom). His administration is credited with advancing civil-service reform, assailing high tariffs, modernizing the navy, and attacking unions.

Conklin Avenue Henry Conklin was a nineteenth-century real estate developer who with J. S. Remsen purchased property from Peter Lott.

Cozine Avenue Farmer Jacob Cozine (1793–1873) was a trustee for Public School 72, for many years the only school in the New Lots farming community. Built with the lumber from trees hewed by Jacob Cozine's father, Garrett Cozine (1760–1845), the school provided an education to members of the Van Sicklen, Schenck, and Rapelye families, among others.

Cypress Hills National Cemetery (625 Jamaica Avenue) New York City's sole national cemetery, it ceased new interments in the 1950s. Although its residents can't rival Green-Wood's, it does boast Jackie Robinson, Lou Gehrig, Edward G. Robinson, Mae West, and—part of its early mandate—several thousand Civil War dead. (See chapter introduction for origin of Cypress Hills.)

Cypress Hills National Cemetery, view from the Heights at Ridgewood

Dewitt Avenue George Dewitt worked in the Brooklyn branch of the Topographical Bureau, an office responsible for laying out new streets and maintaining the borough's official maps. Until 1899, Brooklyn relied on the Bronx-based topographical office, which provided services for Greater New York. But Brooklyn borough president Edward M. Grout advocated for a

Kings County branch to reduce the inefficiencies of sending Brooklyn engineers to the Bronx when decisions about laying streets or sewers had to be made.

Dumont Avenue Named for the Swiss jurist and political writer Pierre Étienne Louis Dumont (1759–1829), who was a close friend of, and speech writer for, French writer Honoré Mirabeau and an early disciple of philosopher Jeremy Bentham.

Elderts Lane Named for the family of Johannes Eldert, one of the original Flatbush settlers who in 1667 received a patent for the land. Near the edge of the city line, the street was colloquially called Enfield, corrupted from Endfield, which referred to its location at the end of the fields of the town.

Erskine Street Known intimately to Brooklyn Dodger fans as "Oisk," Indiana-raised pitcher Carl Erskine (b. 1926) had a career 122–78 record from 1948 to 1959, including two no-hitters.

Folsom Place Folsom was the maiden name of the wife of New Lots party boss Harry H. Adams (d. 1897). Adams served as county treasurer from 1882 to 1895 and was the Democratic leader of Brooklyn's Twenty-sixth Ward. Once known as "Honest Harry" Adams, his final days as treasurer were mired in scandal.

Force Tube Avenue Unlikely to be awarded Most Euphonious Street Name, this unusual Brooklyn moniker refers to the high-pressure water-main lines that once flowed between the Ridgewood Reservoir and the water-pumping station at Conduit Boulevard and Atlantic Avenue. The reservoir operated for over a century and was then used (until 1989) as an emergency water source for Brooklyn and Queens.

Franklin K. Lane High School (999 Jamaica Avenue) Woodrow Wilson's interior secretary, Franklin K. Lane (1864–1921), is best remembered for introducing the National Park Service in 1916. He later swapped his environmental post to become vice president of the Pan-American Petroleum Company. Shortly after his death, Lane's remarkable private letters documenting the passions and inconsistencies of Wilson's war cabinet were published; they included the following dark meditation: "The whole world is skew-jee, awry, distorted and altogether perverse. The President is broken in body and obstinate in spirit. Einstein has declared the law of gravitation outgrown and decadent. Drink, consoling friend of a perturbed world, is shut off; and all goes merry as a dance in hell."

Franklin K. Lane, 1913

Glenmore Avenue Deriving from the Gaelic term meaning "large valley," the street's name likely relates to its topography. Glenmore was once called South Carolina Street.

Hegeman Avenue Adriaen Hegeman (1624–1672), the progenitor of a large Flatbush family, found his way to New Netherland in 1652 from Gelderland, Holland. A farmer, Hegeman was also the schout (sheriff) of four of the five Dutch towns: Nieuw Amersfoort, Breukelen, Midwout, and Nieuw Utrecht and the first schoolmaster in 1659 of the Flatbush Dutch Reformed Church school.

Hendrix Street Ephraim Hendricks, the progenitor of one of East New York's original families, emigrated to New Netherland in 1664. His descendent, Joseph Clifford Hendrix (1853–1904), the likely source for the street's name, was a reporter and editor for the *New York Sun*, president of two banks, and head of the Board of Education. Defeated in the race for Brooklyn mayor in 1883 at the age of thirty, Hendrix was appointed Kings County postmaster by President Grover Cleveland and later elected a one-term Democrat to the 53rd Congress.

Herzl Street Changed from Ames Street in 1913, this Brownsville street is named for Theodore Herzl (1860–1904), the founder of modern Zionism. An Austrian journalist and playwright, Herzl believed that assimilation was destined to fail and that Jews, whom he considered a nation, should have a distinct homeland. Yet Herzl saw the creation of a Jewish state through his own secular lens. It was not to be a religious homeland but rather a safe haven from European anti-Semitism. One might say that the neighborhood of Brownsville—once 70 percent Jewish—came close to fulfilling Herzl's wider aspirations (sovereignty excluded).

Highland Place Likely named after nearby Highland Park, whose "high land" refers to the park's elevated plateau and commanding views. Highland Place was called Dresden Street until 1919, when residents petitioned to change its name amid postwar anti-German sentiment.

Hinsdale Street Elizur B. Hinsdale (1831–1916) served as the general counsel of the Long Island Rail Road (LIRR) and authored the LIRR's first history. A prominent New Yorker of considerable means, he was also implicated in one of the celebrated divorce cases of the day. Elizur's brother, William Hinsdale, accused his wife, Frances, of being unfaithful with both Elizur and Willie Carl, William's clerk. Frances countersued, alleging that William had an adulterous relationship with Carl's mother. The judge ruled against William and granted Frances a divorce. Whether or not the affair between Elizur and his sister-in-law occurred, Elizur's own marriage was annulled on the grounds that his wife was insane.

Jerome Street A New York financier and grandfather of Winston Churchill,

Leonard Jerome (1817–1891) was the founder of the American Academy of Music and at one point an owner of the *New York Times*. Known internationally for his contribution to horse racing, Jerome founded Jerome Park, where the Belmont Stakes had its first run in 1867. His Brooklyn-born daughter, Jennie Jerome, married Sir Randolph Churchill and was the mother of the future British prime minister. Jerome Avenue in the Bronx, the dividing point between the borough's west and east sides, is also named for him.

Kiely Place Named for Monsignor John F. Kiely (1861–1941), Irish-born pastor of the Roman Catholic Church of the Blessed Sacrament on Fulton Street and Euclid Avenue. The street name was changed from Crescent Place in 1937.

Liberty Avenue Liberty Avenue received its name because in contrast to the surrounding toll roads (e.g., Jamaica Avenue), it was a free road.

Lincoln Terrace Park (Rochester, East New York, and Buffalo avenues) Named for the sixteenth president, it was long an immigrant stomping ground and is vividly described in Alfred Kazin's *A Walker in the City*. It was known in Yiddish as *Kitzel*, or "Tickle" Park, a gentle reference to the romantic interludes common there.

Livonia Avenue Originally named Linnington, after early settlers in the area whose land, together with the farms of the Rapelye and Van Sicklen families, constituted the original plots of East New York. The name was later changed to Livonia, after the Russian province. It was on Livonia Avenue that Midnight Rose, a twenty-four-hour candy store, served as headquarters for Murder, Inc. from the 1920s through the 1940s. This group of Italian and Jewish mobsters, formed by notable gangsters Charles "Lucky" Luciano and Meyer Lansky, was responsible for over eight hundred contract killings from New York to California.

Logan Street Volunteer Civil War general John A. Logan (1826–1886) was adamant at the conflict's onset that "the Union must prevail"—this despite his key role in launching Illinois's brutal black codes. Following the war, Logan switched parties, became a leader in the battle to impeach Andrew Johnson, was elected twice to the Senate, and became an unsuccessful vice presidential candidate with James Blaine. Today he is best remembered for his military order establishing Memorial Day.

John A. Logan

Lott Avenue (see Lott Place/Lott Street, chapter 5)

McClancy Place Named Repose Place until 1956, it was renamed to honor Monsignor Joseph McClancy, pastor of St. Gabriel's Church.

Miller Avenue Popular East New York physician and German immigrant Dr. Francis Miller was a founder of the Society of German Physicians of the City of New York. He moved to East New York in 1864, where he also served as a trustee of the East New York Savings Bank. Miller's son Horace played an important role in the development of East New York.

Nehemiah Houses (440 Watkins Street) Built by the East Brooklyn Congregations to provide affordable housing in the neighborhood, the Brooklyn Nehemiah Houses (whose construction began in 1983) were named after the biblical prophet, whose name translates as "God comforts." In the Old Testament, Nehemiah was said to have led the Jews back to Jerusalem in 444 BC to rebuild the city following Babylonian captivity, and his name was thus an inspiring metaphor for church leaders behind the development.

Nichols Avenue Colonel Richard Nicholls became the first British governor of New York in 1664 when the island transferred from Dutch to British rule. With four British frigates at his command, Nicholls seized the land from Peter Stuyvesant without a shot fired and changed New Amsterdam's name to New York. Nicholls took pains to gain New Yorkers' admiration, appointing the well-respected Thomas Willett as mayor and offering protection against religious persecution. The spelling of the Nicholls surname was changed to "Nichols" in the eighteenth century.

Paerdegat Basin Only minorly corrupted from the Dutch, *Paerdegat* derives from *paard/gat* or "horse gate." The name's usage dates from the seventeenth century. There are a series of streets in the area that carry the Paerdegat name.

Pink Houses (2632 Linden Boulevard) Built in 1957 and named for Louis Heaton Pink (1882–1955), chairman of the New York State Housing Board and the person responsible for crafting legislation that created the New York City Housing Authority.

Pitkin Avenue Connecticut dry-goods merchant John R. Pitkin in 1835 began buying farmland in the area from prominent families including the Linningtons, Wyckoffs, and Van Sicklens to develop a metropolitan counterweight to New York. He also set up a shoe factory at the corner of today's Williams Street and Pitkin Avenue. During the Panic of 1837, Pitkin was forced to resell much of his recently purchased land, shattering his dream of a New York rival and prompting his retreat to Woodville, Queens (later Woodhaven), where he had earlier developed a workers' village. Pitkin Avenue was once the center of one of Brooklyn's largest shopping districts, dubbed by locals "Brooklyn's Fifth Avenue."

Powell Street Two-time Brooklyn Democratic mayor Samuel S. Powell (1815–1879), a clothier by trade, during the Civil War effectively defended the Navy

Pitkin Avenue, mid-1950s

Yard from plotting Confederate rebels in what became known as the "Navy Yard Scare." Powell was also elected comptroller and county treasurer. Over the course of Powell's mayoralty, transportation trumped tradition: Brooklyn historian Henry Stiles explained that "during [Powell's] administration, the much debated question as to the advisability of running the street rail road cars on the Sabbath was settled affirmatively, after a fierce contest."

Corner of Powell Street and Livonia Avenue, May 21, 1917

Sackman Street Brothers Jacob H. and Henry Sackman were part of the wave of German immigrants that settled in New Lots in the mid-nineteenth century. Originally from Hamburg, Jacob worked as a bookbinder and later as a land agent in tandem with Andrew Barbey (see entry in this chapter). The first Orthodox synagogue in Brownsville, Beth Hamidrash Hagadol, was organized on the street in 1889. Sackman Street was also home to the Brownsville Labor Lyceum, a lecture hall that served as headquarters for the Socialist Party and as a political and cultural center for the working-class community.

Schenck Avenue First settler Jan Martense Schenk (d. 1689) in 1675 built the Schenk homestead, which three centuries later was disassembled and rebuilt within the Brooklyn Museum. Descendents were spread out over the county and maintained landholdings in Bushwick, New Lots, Flatlands, and Flatbush. Schenck Avenue is likely named for Judge Teunis Schenck (1762–1842), who owned the land from Schenck Avenue to Warwick Street and with twelve slaves was one of Flatbush's largest slaveowners. By the fourth generation in America, an additional "c" was added to the name. There is also a Schenck Court at the northern end of Schenck Avenue and a Schenck Street in Canarsie.

Schroeders Avenue Brooklyn Republican mayor Frederick A. Schroeder (1833–1899) during his tenure in office (1876–77) oversaw several prominent firsts: the Brooklyn Bridge's initial wiring, Ocean Parkway's opening, and the construction of Brooklyn's first elevated railroad. A German American, Schroeder also founded the Germania Savings Bank to help other Germans better manage their money. His expertise was used for wider purposes when he became city comptroller in 1871. Once labeled a "reformer before reform was a fetish," Schroeder limited the role of the Board of Aldermen in confirming nominations, thereby reducing back-room deals. While serving in the state senate, Schroeder worked to institutionalize his anticorruption advocacy by vesting all power to appoint heads of city departments with the mayor.

Sheffield Avenue This street was named in honor of British nobleman John Sheffield, Duke of Buckingham and Normanby (1647–1721). Known as Lord Mulgrave (he was the son of Edmund second Earl of Mulgrave), Sheffield was a statesman, soldier, poet, and essayist. While he famously averred, "Learn to write well or not to write at all," he is better remembered for building Buckingham Palace in 1703. (The royal family purchased it later in the century.)

Snediker Avenue Patriarch Jan Snedeker (1609–1679) came to New Amsterdam before 1640 from the Duchy of Oldenburg, Germany, and later received a deed to land in Midwout from Peter Stuyvesant. He served as magistrate and later pastor at the Flatbush Dutch Reformed Church. Scion John I. Snedeker was renowned in the 1830s for the Snedeker Hotel, a favorite for horsemen like himself and around which the Cypress Hills settlement formed. The date of the family name's corruption is undetermined, though there are 126 known spellings of the original name including "Schniddekker."

Spring Creek Towers (formerly Starrett City) Covering 153 acres and including forty-six apartment buildings, this complex is the country's largest federally subsidized housing project. The Starrett Corporation, a major real estate developer and builder, is responsible for many significant metropolitan-area projects including the Empire State Building, 40 Wall Street, and the classic Starrett-Lehigh Building on 21st Street and Tenth Avenue, with its miles of banded windows. Col. William A. Starrett (1877–1932), the firm's progenitor, directed the construction of some two hundred buildings, in the process transforming New York's skyline.

Opened in 1974, Starrett City became notorious for instituting quotas and screening applicants based on race (this was later challenged in court). The name was changed in 2002, though most still call the complex by its original designation.

Stanley Avenue Originally named for the early Dutch settler Stoothoff family, the name was changed to honor journalist Sir Henry Morton Stanley (1841–1904), who on assignment for the *New York Herald* went to Africa to search for the missionary Dr. David Livingstone. When he found the ailing explorer, it was Stanley who offered the famous line "Dr. Livingstone, I presume?" Stanley's real name is unknown—he took the name Henry Stanley from a merchant who befriended him when he moved to New Orleans at age fifteen.

Strauss Street Like Strauss Park on Manhattan's Upper West Side and Strauss Square on the Lower East Side, this street is named for the Bavarian-born Strauss family. Brothers Nathan and Isidor Strauss purchased R. H. Macy's department store in 1896 after working there for two decades. A one-term congressman from New York and a noted philanthropist, Isidor was a close adviser to President Grover Cleveland. In 1912 he died with his wife, Ida, on the *Titanic*. During a U.S. Senate inquiry on the sinking of the ship it was revealed that Ida had a chance to survive by evacuating on a lifeboat with other women and children but chose to remain with her husband. She was reported to have said, "We have been living together for forty years and where you go, I go." Over forty thousand people attended their memorial service.

Sutter Avenue The avenue commemorates Peter "Pete" D. Sutter (d. 1892), Brooklyn Democratic boss of the Twenty-sixth Ward and in 1878 one of three appointed police commissioners in New Lots. The street had been called Union Avenue until 1887.

Thatford Avenue New Lots resident Gilbert Sayre Thatford (1822–1902) spent his professional hours engaging in real estate transactions and developing a wholesale and retail coal business in the 1870s. He was also one of the founders of the First Congregational Church of New Lots, dedicated in 1869 on a plot of land donated by Thatford himself. He lived nearby on what was called Black Stump Road, today's 73rd Avenue in Queens.

Vanderveer Street (see Vanderveer Place, chapter 5)

Van Siclen Avenue Named for the Van Sicklens (though minus the "k"), one of the earliest seventeenth-century Dutch farming dynasties in Flatbush and Gravesend. (Gravesend's Van Sicklen Street retains the "k.")

Van Siclen farmhouse at 569 New Lots Avenue, north side
between Van Siclen Avenue and Hendrix Street, 1924

Van Sinderen Avenue Family patriarch Ulpianus Van Sinderen (1672–1753) emigrated from Holland in 1746 to serve as the pastor of the Flatbush Dutch Reformed Church. His grandson, Hotse Van Sinderen, for whom the street is likely named, moved to New Lots in 1823. The Van Sinderen estate was one of the farms purchased and developed into Brownsville. Adriaen Van Sinderen, Hotse's son, was president of a number of prominent Brooklyn organizations including the Brooklyn Temperance Society, the Long Island Bible Society, and the Brooklyn chapter of the American Colonization Society (an organization supporting black emigration to West Africa).

Van Sinderen Avenue and
Fulton Street, 1912

Varkens Hook Road A seventeenth-century remnant, the street has had various monikers over the years but by 1849 took on its current name. *Varken* is Dutch for "pig," and, as with Red Hook or Yellow Hook (Bay Ridge), "hook" likely derives from *hoek,* or "corner." In any case, it is a fair assumption that a pig farm was once in the vicinity.

Woodson Houses (403 Powell Street) Carter G(odson) Woodson (1875–1950), the son and grandson of slaves, was one of the preeminent scholars of African American history during his lifetime. In 1916 Woodson founded the Association for the Study of Negro Life, an organization that issued the scholarly publication *Journal of Negro History* (in 2002 it became the *Journal for African-American History*). Woodson received degrees from both the University of Chicago and Harvard and was a prolific writer, publishing on migration patterns of African Americans and other themes. His best-known work, *The Mis-Education of the Negro,* discusses in detail the problematic nature of American education as it affects the black community.

Wortman Avenue John S. Wortman, a landowner in New Lots, was a blacksmith whose shop was attached to his home on New Lots Road near Van Siclen Avenue.

Zion Triangle (Legion Street, Pitkin Avenue, and East New York Avenue) Donated by landowner Peter Vanderveer and known as Vanderveer Park, it was renamed Zion Park in 1911 for the city of Jerusalem. It became Loews Square in 1930, after the Loews Pitkin Theatre, but regained the Zion tag (now as a triangle) in 1997.

7 | Southwest Brooklyn

Bath Beach, Bay Ridge–Fort Hamilton, Bensonhurst, Dyker Heights

A map of Southwest Brooklyn appears on the following pages.

Fort Hamilton residents, mid-1980s

The neighborhoods covered in this chapter were once part of New Utrecht, one of the six original Kings County towns. Longstanding Native American land of the Canarsee and Nyack tribes, Dutch West India Company director Cornelis Van Werckhoven received permission from Governor Stuyvesant to settle the area, conditional on his bringing one hundred settlers to the colony (the Company had already claimed title to the land via a previous purchase from the local Nyacks). Planning to reside there after a return trip to the Netherlands, Werckhoven unexpectedly died, and the person whom he had hired to tutor his children, Huguenot Jacques Cortelyou (1625–1693), now also became responsible for his property. Cortelyou named the area Nieuw Utrecht in honor of Werckhoven's place of origin and petitioned New Amsterdam to divide the land into lots. The British retained the Utrecht name, only anglicizing Nieuw to New, and the area remained independent until it was incorporated as Brooklyn's Thirtieth Ward in 1894.

On the southwestern side lies Bay Ridge, called Yellow Hook until 1853 (the name dating back to at least the 1670s), perhaps for the yellow color of the clay that leached onto the shore (and contrasting with the red clay of Red Hook). The name's appeal plummeted with the yellow fever epidemic of the late 1840s. When local residents gathered to identify an alternative, florist James Weir suggested Bay Ridge—dually topographical, as it described both the area's glacial ridge and its location at the upper point of New York Bay. The adjoining Fort Hamilton, which replaced the previous Fort Lewis, built in 1812 to protect the narrows around Gravesend Bay, is named for the founding father Alexander Hamilton.

Located on the shore of Gravesend Bay, the Bath Beach neighborhood was once one of Kings County's elite seaside locales. (The beach was also the late-August 1776 British landing site, the prelude to the Battle of Brooklyn.) Destroyed by the WPA-era Shore Parkway and then landfilled (to the south) with the excavated aftermath of the Verrazano-Narrows Bridge, the area no longer immediately suggests its original name, that of the hot-springs-rich town of Bath, England.

Still in the 1880s, parts of Bath Beach remained farmland largely controlled by members of the Benson family. Inspired by the lucrative Bath Beach resorts and the emergence of trolley service and steam rail into Kings County's nether reaches, developer James Lynch sought to buy out the Benson clan. It is said that the Benson family requested that the new development bear their surname as a condition to sell their land. Purchased in 1889, the soon-to-be-exclusive community was for a short time called by the more resort-connoting Bensonhurst-by-the-Sea before adopting its current name: Bensonhurst.

Sandwiched between Bay Ridge–Fort Hamilton and Bensonhurst lies the neighborhood of Dyker Heights. Attribution of the name has been given to the Dutch farmers who built dikes to drain the area's wetland; others believe the name is of more recent vintage since as late as the 1920s real estate auctions were calling the area Bay Ridge East.

Barkaloo Cemetery (Narrows Avenue and MacKay Place) Founded by Jacques Barkaloo and originally a family homestead cemetery, it is the smallest graveyard in Brooklyn. Barkaloo's great-granddaughter, Lemma Barkaloo (1840–1870), was both the country's first female law student and the first woman to try a case in court, before her young life was cut short.

Battery Avenue This avenue refers to Fort Hamilton's nearby battery, defined as a grouping of artillery pieces defending the shoreline.

Bennet-Farrell House (119 95th Street off Shore Road) With the Howard E. and Jessie Jones House (see entry in this chapter), it is one of only two landmarked houses in the area. Built ca. 1847 and moved here in 1913, this Greek Revival villa bears the name of original landowning resident Joseph S. Bennet and, after 1890, of businessman and Tammany Hall clubhouse politician James T. Farrell.

Bennett Court Named for the Bennet (later Bennett) family, major landowners in the area. Patriarch Willem Adrianse Bennet acquired with Jacques Bentyn approximately nine hundred acres of land in 1626 from 24th Street to 60th Street in one of the first real estate deals recorded in the county. Scion and poet-historian Gertrude Ryder Bennett Williams until her death in 1982 lived in the Wyckoff-Bennett homestead on Kings Highway and East 22nd Street (see chapter 6).

Benson Avenue A member of a prominent landholding family for whom Bensonhurst was named, Egbert Benson (1746–1833) was New York State's first attorney general, chief justice of the New York Supreme Court, and Federalist representative to the U.S. Congress. First president of the New-York Historical Society, Benson also published *A Memoir on Dutch Names of Places*.

His namesake nephew, Egbert (1789–1866), in 1820 married Jane Cowenhoven (1803–1867), who inherited much of the property in the area.

Bergen Place Longstanding New Utrecht resident Teunis Bergen (1806–1881) was a surveyor and farmer with Dutch as his mother tongue. Bergen was from 1836 to 1859 the supervisor of New Utrecht and a one-term Democratic representative in the U.S. Congress. A local historian, he is also considered the father of Brooklyn genealogy. (See chapter 3 for more.)

Bliss Terrace Manufacturer Eliphalet Williams Bliss (1836–1903) went from being an apprentice in an upstate New York machine shop to owning and operating both the E. W. Bliss Company and the United States Projectile Company, large-scale operations that developed the means of mass production for the pressed-metal trade. Among others, the E. W. Bliss Company provided material used in the building of the Brooklyn Bridge. Bliss was also well known for the various positions he held, including vice president of the Brooklyn Heights Railroad and director of the Brooklyn Gas Fixture Company. Owl's Head, his well-known Bay Ridge estate purchased from Henry C. Murphy, was later transformed into Owl's Head Park (see entry in this chapter).

Cristoforo Colombo Boulevard (Eighteenth Avenue between Ocean Parkway and 86th Street) The Italian explorer would have approved of the spelling of his name here (and it makes up for the borough's flub with Verrazzano). The boulevard is a secondary designation for Eighteenth Avenue and is often considered New York's authentic Little Italy (though Arthur Avenue in the Bronx might have something to say about that).

Cropsey Avenue Named for the early landholding Cropsey family, one of the first to settle in New Utrecht. Eighteenth-century German-speaking immigrant Casper Crepser married in succession two sisters of Jacques Barkaloo's (see entry in this chapter); the name was altered to Cropsy and later Cropsey. Descendents have included Hudson River School painter Jasper Cropsey (1823–1900); Teunis Bergen's successor as town supervisor, militia colonel William J. Cropsey; James "Boss" Cropsey (1785–1861), who supervised the construction of the New Utrecht Reformed Church; and murderer Andrew Bergen Cropsey, who in 1908 killed his wife in an act of jealousy in their Bath Beach home. His terse comments afterward are worthy of Dostoevsky: "I did a rash act. I am sorry. I suppose I'll go to the electric chair."

Dahlgren Place Named for John Adolphus Bernard Dahlgren (1809–1870), U.S. Navy officer from Philadelphia who became head of the Washington Navy Yard at the outbreak of the Civil War. Promoted to rear admiral, he was a confidant of Lincoln's and aided in the 1864 taking of Savannah and the 1865 siege of Charleston. Dahlgren developed various weapons including the famous "Dahlgren gun," a standard armament on navy ships during the Civil War.

Duryea Court This early Kings County landed elite family originated with Joost Durie (George Duryea), a Dutch Huguenot who settled in New Utrecht in the seventeenth century. Moving his family from New Utrecht in 1861 to what is now Greenpoint, he built a home on Meeker Avenue that is the only remaining homestead of early settlers to this area. Once the Duryeas no longer resided there, the home was occupied by Josiah Blackwell, for whom Blackwell's Island, now Roosevelt Island, is named. There is also a Duryea Place in Flatbush.

Flagg Court (7200 Ridge Boulevard between 72nd and 73rd streets) A bold and creative venture in affordable housing, this mid-1930s 422-unit apartment complex was designed by and named after the master architect Ernest Flagg (1857–1947). Flagg was known for decrying the iniquities of tenement living and sought to identify innovative ways to house the multitude. Once upon a time, the premises of Flagg Court maintained a swimming pool, bowling alley, tennis court, community playhouse, and bow-and-arrow range. Flagg's Lower Manhattan Singer Building (demolished in 1968) was the tallest building in the world ever to be destroyed until the World Trade Center catastrophe in 2001.

Flagg Court, 2005

Fontbonne Hall Academy (Shore Road and 99th Street) Purchased by her longtime companion Diamond Jim Brady, it was once the home of Lillian Russell, a prominent actress and operetta singer of the late nineteenth and early twentieth centuries. When the Sisters of St. Joseph acquired the mansion in 1937, it was named to honor Mother Saint John Fontbonne, who refounded the congregation in Lyon in 1807 after being spared the guillotine during the French Revolution. The Academy is now a private girls' school and is one of the few remaining mansions in the area. The building is one of several for the school.

Fort Hamilton Named for *Federalist Papers* author and first secretary of the treasury Alexander Hamilton (ca. 1755–1804) and designed by Simon Bernard (1779–1839), a former aide to Napoleon, Fort Hamilton (completed in 1831) is New York's only active military post and installation. Military figures stationed here in the antebellum period have included Robert E. Lee (for five years), Stonewall Jackson, and Abner Doubleday. At this site, on

August 23, 1776, the British landed, sixteen thousand persons strong, at the onset of the Revolutionary War.

Giuseppe Garibaldi

Garibaldi Park (Eighteenth Avenue between 82nd and 83rd streets) Revolutionary hero of Italian unification and the father of modern Italy, Giuseppe Garibaldi (1807–1882) mobilized thousands of volunteers to free the peninsula from Spanish, French, and Austrian control. Prior to his continental exploits, off and on between 1850 and 1854 Garibaldi shared a home on Staten Island with inventor Antonio Meucci (see chapter 8) and worked at Meucci's candle factory.

Gatling Place The "Gatling gun" of Richard Jordan Gatling (1818–1903), a rapid-fire machine gun, became world renowned at the same period in the 1860s that this street was laid. Originally called Monmouth Street, Fort Hamilton's proximity explains the street's renaming.

Gelston Avenue Scion George S. Gelston's (1805–1891) sizable 1847 land purchase in the neighboring environs is the source of the street's name. Gelston lived on Shore Road and Third Avenue.

Harway Avenue Nineteenth-century real estate developer James L. Harway established the Harway Development Corporation and was a large property owner in the area.

Howard E. and Jessie Jones House (Narrows Avenue and 83rd Street) Better known as the Gingerbread House—"black forest art nouveau" according to the American Institute of Architects (AIA) guide—it is one of the finest examples of the Arts and Crafts movement in the metropolitan area. An official New York City landmark, it was built for shipping merchant Howard E. Jones and his family and finished in 1917.

Howard E. and Jessie Jones House, 2005

John J. Carty Park (Fort Hamilton Parkway and 94–95th streets) Named for John J. Carty (1908–1970), municipal-finance expert and first deputy comptroller (under three administrations). A Bay Ridge resident, Carty was a protégé of Brooklyn clubhouse politician, comptroller, and mayor Abe Beame.

John Paul Jones Park (Shore Road, Fourth Avenue, 101st Street, and Fort Hamilton Parkway) Every school kid knows "Father of the American Navy" John Paul Jones's (1747–1792) Revolutionary War *cri de coeur*: "I have not yet begun to fight." His reputation is less estimable to the British, who long considered him a pirate. (Disraeli wrote that "the nurses of Scotland hushed their crying charges by the whisper of his name.") Still, Jones's early American triumphs served him well, and on Thomas Jefferson's recommendation, Empress Catherine II invited him to Russia. Transformed into Rear Admiral "Pavel Ivanovich Jones," he fought alongside Prince Potemkin against the Turks in the Black Sea Campaign. Despite successes, his alleged molestation of a ten-year-old in St. Petersburg hastened his departure, and he soon died from pneumonia in France. For over a century, Jones lay in an unmarked French grave, until the naval jingoism of Teddy Roosevelt prompted a search that helped unearth Jones's remains in 1905. None other than the USS *Brooklyn* returned his body to America.

Locals frequently call the park by its nickname, Cannonball Park, for the Civil War–era Rodman gun, a cast-iron cannon weighing in excess of one thousand pounds. One of the few remaining examples is situated here, steps from its original placement at Fort Hamilton.

John Paul Jones Park/Cannonball Park, mid-1980s

Lapskaus Boulevard (Eighth Avenue) During its twentieth-century Scandinavian heyday, the avenue was commonly called Lapskaus Boulevard, after the salted Norwegian beef stew. In fact, the Bay Ridge neighborhood (with parts of Sunset Park) once had the largest concentration of Norwegians in the world outside Norway. When scores of buildings were destroyed in the early 1960s to make way for the Verrazano-Narrows Bridge a longstanding resident lamented that it "knocked the heart out of the Norwegian community."

Lapskaus Boulevard, 1961

Leif Ericson Park and Square (between 66th and 67th streets from Fourth Avenue to Fort Hamilton Parkway) Thought by some to be the first European to enter North America, the Great Norse soldier Leif Ericson (ca. 985–1020) is for Norwegians a key historical figure. Naming this park for him underscores the longstanding influence of the population in Bay Ridge, once home to a variety of Norwegian cultural and commercial institutions. (At one point, Bay Ridge High School was the only New York City school to offer Norwegian-language courses.) The sixteen-acre park continues to be the terminus of Norway's Constitution Day celebration every May with the crowning of "Miss Norway."

Liberty Pole Boulevard (84th Street and Eighteenth Avenue) The boulevard, a part of 84th Street, commemorates the liberty pole adjacent to the New

Utrecht Reformed Church, the sixth liberty pole to stand on the site. Originally erected in late 1783 at the Revolutionary War's conclusion to celebrate the British departure, the liberty pole (often a ship's mast) represented to colonists a symbol of defiance to British oppression. The Georgian Gothic Revival New Utrecht Reformed Church is one of New York City's first land-marked buildings.

MacKay Place Irish immigrant and Bay Ridge resident John W. MacKay (d. 1902) struck it rich in the gold hills of the West in 1849 and ventured into the real estate, mining, and telegraph businesses, establishing the Commercial Cable Company. A prominent landholder residing on the elite Shore Road in New Utrecht, MacKay was also active in Democratic Party reform politics. In a widely covered news story, John MacKay's granddaughter was secretly married in 1926 to Irving Berlin, against the will of her father, MacKay's son Clarence. Despite her father's hostility, Ellin (MacKay) Berlin went on to have four daughters with the composer and was the subject of the great Berlin ballad "Always."

McKinley Park (73rd Street, Seventh Avenue, 78th Street, and Fort Hamilton Parkway) America's third president to be assassinated, Ohio Republican William McKinley (1843–1901) was just months into his second term when he was killed in Buffalo. Elected by interests partial to high tariffs, his time in office was dominated by foreign policy—the "New Imperialism"—notably the Spanish-American War. The $500 bill, whose tenure lasted from 1928 to 1946, carried his face. The park was named two years after his passing.

Milestone Park (81st Street and Eighteenth Avenue) The oldest mile marker still in existence, the 1741 three-foot-high indicator marked the intersection of Kings Highway and Old New Utrecht Road (Eighteenth Avenue today). The milestone is a granite replica; the sandstone original resides in the Brooklyn Historical Society.

New Utrecht Avenue The long avenue takes its name from the original Dutch town (see introduction to this chapter). Once known as the Brooklyn, Greenwood, and Bath Plank Road, it was the project of a private company that received approval for its construction in 1852. In 1864, it formed part of the right-of-way for New Utrecht's first steam-powered rail line, the Brooklyn, Bath, and Coney Island, the ancestor of the BMT's West End line (now the D train). There are only a handful of vestiges of the name remaining in the area, including the 1827 New Utrecht Re-formed Church on 84th Street and Eighteenth Avenue and New Utrecht High School on 80th Street and Sixteenth Avenue (of which Sandy Koufax is an alumnus).

Oliver Street Named for the family of Mary Van Duzen Oliver, a nineteenth-century property owner, the street appeared on maps ca. 1875.

Ovington Avenue/Ovington Court The broad street and court were named by the Ovington Village Association, a cohort of fifty artists who in 1850 purchased the Ovington family farm. Charles Parsons, the art director at the largest publisher in the United States, Harper and Brothers, was the association's president. Other members included Otto Heinigke, a stained-glass specialist responsible for the windows of Bay Ridge Dutch Reformed Church, and lithographer George Schlegel. Writer and civil rights

Mary White Ovington, 1902

activist Mary White Ovington (1865–1951), a descendent of the original family, was born to Brooklyn abolitionists, would summer at her family's Bay Ridge property, and in 1909 became one of the founders of the NAACP.

Owl's Head Park (Colonial Road and Wakeman Place) Once part of Henry C. Murphy's estate situated along the glacial ridge, the origin of the name of this twenty-seven-acre park is contested. Some contend that the owl heads fronting the gates of the driveway are the source of the name; others submit that the land's shape is reflective of an owl; still others claim that owls once graced the area. The land became parkland after final owner Eliphalet Bliss's widow died (locals usually refer to it as Bliss Park). In 1937, Robert Moses created the park we see today.

Parrott Place Similar to the military-connoting parallel streets of Gatling Place, Dahlgren Place, and Battery Avenue in neighboring Fort Hamilton, Parrott Place refers to Robert Parker Parrott (1804–1877), an inventor of the projectile and cannon that carry his name.

Perry Terrace Arriving in Bay Ridge in 1851, landowner Joseph A. Perry (d. 1881) was an investor in the ferry business and chiefly responsible for the founding of Christ Church. Perry is best known for his important contributions to Green-Wood Cemetery during its first decades. Perry lived on Bay Ridge Avenue near Ridge Boulevard; his family eventually sold the lot in 1895 to the new nonvolunteer fire department.

Poly Place Named associatively for the adjacent Polytechnic Preparatory Country Day School, a prep school founded in 1854 and a former part of the Brooklyn Collegiate and Polytechnic Institute on Livingston Street. It moved here in 1916.

St. Bernadette's Church (8201 Thirteenth Avenue at 83rd Street) St. Bernadette, the Lourdes saint to whom the Virgin Mary is said to have appeared, was canonized in 1933. The church itself has a replica grotto to depict the scene of the miraculous apparition.

St. Finbar's Church (138 Bay 20th Street) This Roman Catholic church honors St. Finbar (d. ca. 633), patron of immigrants. He founded a monastery and became its first bishop in an area that would develop into the city of Cork, Ireland. He was named by monks *Fionnbharr,* or "white head," for his light hair.

St. John's Episcopal Church (9818 Fort Hamilton Parkway) Commonly known as the Church of the Generals, this congregation from 1834 has long served the garrison at Fort Hamilton army base and wider community. Stonewall Jackson was baptized here in 1849, and Robert E. Lee served as vestryman from 1842 to 1844. The building is not the church's first and dates from 1890.

Sedgwick Place The Sedgwicks were notable landowners in the area; Theodore Sedgwick was a founding member of the Vestry at Christ Church in Bay Ridge in the 1850s.

Senator Street Esteemed New Utrecht resident Henry Cruse Murphy (1810–1882) is veiled behind this Bay Ridge street name. During his six-term tenure, State Senator Murphy was responsible for pushing through legislation that resulted in the construction of the Brooklyn Bridge. (Boss Tweed provided assistance in procuring the legislative charter, for a modest $65,000 fee.) Prior to this, Murphy had been an owner and editor at the *Brooklyn Daily Eagle,* Brooklyn mayor (at the age of thirty-one), and two-term congressman who supported free trade and opposed the annexation of Texas. As a dark-horse candidate, he came amazingly close to taking the 1852 Democratic presidential nomination—the closest a Brooklynite has come to the Oval Office. Murphy was an avid book collector and an original founder of the Long Island Historical Society (today's Brooklyn Historical Society). He lived for many years in an estate on 67th Street and Colonial Road, where Owl's Head Park stands today.

Senator Street and Third Avenue, 1940

Seth Low Playground (Bay Parkway, Avenue P and West 12th Street) Mayor and university president Seth Low (1850–1916) started out professionally in his father's richly successful tea and silk importing business. Venturing into politics, he was twice elected Brooklyn mayor (1882–86), where he pushed reform of the civil service, public finance, and education. While Columbia University's president from 1890 to 1901, Low oversaw its move to a new Morningside Heights campus and helped in the university's administrative reorganization. He subsequently served as the second mayor of consolidated New York from 1901 to 1903.

Seth Low, ca. 1901

Shore Parkway Dedicated in 1940, it is the southern link to what is commonly called the Belt Parkway, which rings the shorefront of Brooklyn. Robert Moses's proposed parkway was originally called the "Marginal Boulevard," a name thankfully dropped, and later the "Circumferential Parkway," a clunky title jettisoned after a decade of use. The parkway's construction cleared the area once home to Canarsie's legendary amusement park Golden City, a venue at which one could gawk at the four-horned goat, among other attractions.

Shore Parkway, 1970s

Ulmer Park Library (2602 Bath Avenue at Twenty-sixth Avenue) One of Brooklyn Public Library's many neighborhood branches, this one takes its name from William Ulmer, founder of Bushwick's Ulmer Brewery, who in 1893 opened Ulmer Park, a large resort by Gravesend Bay. In addition to the rifle range, carousel, vaudeville, and dancing, Ulmer Park was known for its German singing festivals, a likely product of Ulmer's Prussian heritage.

Verrazano-Narrows Bridge

In the 1950s members of the Staten Island Chamber of Commerce thought they had a winning argument for the naming of what was called during construction the Narrows Bridge: "Why should there be a Brooklyn, Bronx, Queensboro and Manhattan Bridge and not a Staten Island Bridge?" they asked. The trouble was that the Italian Historical Society had other plans. Under the passionate advocacy of John LaCorte, Florentine explorer Giovanni da Verrazzano (1485–1528), the first European reported to have entered New York Harbor (a full eighty years before Henry Hudson), was proposed to be an ideal candidate for the namesake of the new bridge. Despite Staten Islanders' protests ("a foreigner who made a navigational mistake") and the analogous efforts by the Scandinavian community to name it the Leif Ericson Bridge, endorsements of Verrazano from former governor Averell Harriman and Governor Nelson Rockefeller proved decisive. (The fact that seven thousand people were displaced by the bridge's construction, many of them Italians, may have affected Rockefeller's calculus.) In the end "Narrows" was kept in the name, referring to the winnowing point between the upper and lower bays, and the full name became the Verrazano-Narrows Bridge. Upon the decision, the New York Times boldly predicted that Verrazano would never catch on and that the bridge would be forever known as the "Narrows Bridge," just as the "Thruway Bridge" would always trump the formal "Tappan Zee." Wrong they were. As for Verrazano's spelling, it should of course have a second "z," and the Italian ambassador and Harriman favored such, but Rockefeller backed the Americanized version.

Vincent Gardenia Boulevard Sixteenth Avenue between 86th Street and Shore Parkway was secondarily named in 1993 for the comedian, film star, and Bath Beach native. Gardenia (1922–1992) is known for his Oscar-nominated supporting role in *Bang the Drum Slowly,* his Emmy-winning role as Archie Bunker's neighbor Frank Lorenzo, and his Tony-winning part in *The Prisoner of Second Avenue.*

Wakeman Place Attorney Abram Wakeman (1824–1889) was postmaster general under Lincoln, a one-term Whig representative, and a key person in the formation of the Republican Party. Following his political career, he turned to railroads and helped finance and organize the Bay Ridge and Manhattan Beach lines and develop the hotel resorts on Coney Island, before selling them off to Austin Corbin (see chapter 8).

Wallaston Court Named for the Wallaston Realty Company, which owned property in the 1920s.

Verrazano-Narrows Bridge, 2005

**Bergen Beach, Brighton Beach,
Coney Island, Flatlands,
Gerritsen Beach, Gravesend,
Manhattan Beach, Marine Park,
Mill Basin, Sheepshead Bay**

*A map of Southeastern and
Southern Brooklyn appears
on the following pages.*

Coney Island, 1983

O f the six original seventeenth-century settlements in what is today Brooklyn, only one has specifically English roots: Gravesend. Receiving formal sanction from Dutch governor William Kieft in 1645, it was founded and planned by the remarkable English refugee and religious-freedom advocate Lady Deborah Moody.

Gravesend's derivation has been attributed to several sources: some say Kieft named it after his hometown of s'Gravenzande, Holland (a few actually believe Moody herself named it for Kieft's hometown to curry favor); others contend the origin was Gravesend in Kent, England, Moody's point of debarkation to the Massachusetts Bay Colony. (She spent several years in New England trying unsuccessfully to practice her radical Protestantism.)

Part of the original town of Gravesend, Coney Island existed as common land until portions of it were divided in 1677. The Canarsee had populated its westernmost section, a settlement they called *Narriockh*, meaning "a point of land." The name "Conyne Island" appears in Gravesend's 1645 patent, but like Gravesend itself, its origin is not fully certain. The received wisdom today maintains that the name was a Dutch attempt to reflect the large number of wild rabbits, *konijn*, inhabiting the island.

Austin Corbin of the Corbin Banking Company developed Coney Island's neighbor Manhattan Beach. Moving to the area in 1873, Corbin began speculating on land at the easternmost point of the island, then called Sedge Bank, and within two years had bought out the property and renamed it Manhattan Beach (after that other major island nearby). Corbin and real estate developer Joseph Day subdivided the area into residential lots and acrostically named the blocks from Amherst Street to Quentin Street, interrupted only by Ocean Avenue between Exeter and Falmouth. They hoped the streets' monikers, from place-names in England, would add an air of sophistication to the neighborhood.

Manhattan Beach's neighbor to the west, Brighton Beach, is named for Brighton, England, a seaside resort town. Real estate magnate William

Engeman, who developed the area in 1868, sold his beachfront property to the East River and Coney Island Railroad, which built a hotel at the train's ocean terminus. The railroad's directors named it the Hotel Brighton for the British resort, and the beach became known as Brighton Beach. Like Manhattan Beach, many of the streets—Amherst, Beaumont, and Coleridge, for example—suggest a British elitism that the developers attempted to cultivate.

North of Brighton Beach, hotelier Benjamin Freeman named the shore community of Sheepshead Bay, and in 1844 established the area's first hotel, the Sheepshead. The name is for the large sheepshead salt-water fish that were once in abundance in the nearby bay, its teeth said to resemble those of sheep.

Sandwiched between Sheepshead Bay and Marine Park lies the quiet fishing village of Gerritsen Beach. The neighborhood was named for the early Dutch settler Wolphert Gerritsen, who received a land grant from the Dutch West India Company in 1636. The Gerritsen family had milling concerns for multiple generations; by the 1890s their flour and tide mills ceased operation and were eventually sold to William C. Whitney, who used the land for training race horses.

The neighborhood of Marine Park, settled in the 1650s by Johannes Lott, acquired its nautical name by the 1920s, when the federal government designated the area around Jamaica Bay the future site of what was to be the largest port in the world. The Depression, however, short-circuited the port development plan, and, as was feared, New Jersey took the lead in sea commerce. The land for the park came partially from a 1917 gift to the city from Charles Pratt's son Frederick and housing pioneer Alfred Treadway White.

The Canarsee Indians provided the original name of adjacent neighborhood Mill Basin: *Equandito,* or "Broken Land." The land was sold first to John Tilton Jr. and Samuel Spicer and later to Jan Martense Schenk. Mills were built using the tidal creeks, hence the adopted name. Neighboring Bergen Beach, like a host of other place-names in Brooklyn, takes its name from the Bergen family; it had been Bergen Island until the mid-nineteenth century, when it was adjoined to the main island through landfill.

Flatlands, the name a reflection of the prevailing topography, had earlier been called Nieuw Amersfoort when chartered as one of the original Dutch towns in 1647. Nieuw Amersfoort was named for a town near Utrecht, the Netherlands; the British bestowed on it the less attention-grabbing designation.

Abe Stark Skating Rink and Convention Hall (Surf Avenue, West 19th Street, Boardwalk) This skating rink and convention hall is one of several Brooklyn venues named for the businessman and former Brooklyn borough president Abe Stark (1894–1972). Known as "Mr. Brooklyn," Stark had owned a successful Brownsville men's clothing store for almost four decades and was renowned for his marketing promotions: a famous sign under the Ebbets Field scoreboard in right-center field enticed batters with "Hit Sign, Win Suit." (Mel Ott of the rival New York Giants was the first—and second—batter to succeed.) Stark developed sufficient political influence to later become city council president followed by borough president, from 1962 to 1970.

Asser Levy (Seaside) Park (West 5th Street and Surf Avenue) One of the twenty-three Jews who first set foot in New Amsterdam in 1654, Asser Levy (d. 1681) fled from Brazil when Portugal recaptured portions of the country formerly under Dutch colonial control. While the new immigrants escaped possible inquisition, they instead faced Peter Stuyvesant, no friend to the non–Dutch Reform, who asked the Dutch West India Company for the right to expel them. The appeal was rejected after the refugees petitioned fellow Jews in Holland to speak out on their behalf. One year later, Levy figured prominently in another pitched battle with Stuyvesant. After Stuyvesant refused to let Jews serve in the volunteer army (instead imposing a tax on them), Levy filed suit with the Dutch West India Company. He won his case, though unlikely from a display of religious amity; that a number of Jews were large-scale investors in the Dutch West India Company probably proved decisive in the end.

Babi Yar Triangle (Corbin Place, Brighton 14th Street, and Oceanview Avenue) A ravine outside Kiev, Ukraine, Babi Yar is the site of a Nazi killing field where thirty-four thousand victims, primarily Jews, were summarily executed over a thirty-six-hour period in September 1941. The area was later used to slaughter some one hundred thousand additional persons including Roma, prisoners of war, and the disabled. Using slave labor over a six-week period in 1943, all evidence of the devastation was eliminated.

Batchelder Street Surveying Gravesend in the 1870s, the land commissioner hired as support a number of persons who would become beneficiaries of street names over the course of their work. Real estate speculator Howard A. Batchelder was one. Also honored were A. L. Ford, G. P. Coyle, F. S. Bragg, E. D. Brigham, and S. Knapp.

Billings Place Probably named for Josh Billings, a close friend of William Whitney (see entry in this chapter) and one of his favorite jockeys. Like several other small streets in the area, it was built on the site of the former Gravesend Race Track.

Bokee Court Attorney and Whig congressman David A(lexander) Bokee (1805–1860) was appointed naval officer of customs of the Port of New York by Millard Fillmore in 1851. Bokee also served as president of the Brooklyn Board of Aldermen and was an unsuccessful candidate for Brooklyn mayor in 1843 (he lost by 311 votes to Joseph Sprague).

Bouck Court Democrat William C. Bouck (1786–1859) was New York's first farmer-governor (1843–45) and for nearly twenty years the state's canal commissioner. Perhaps not by coincidence, Bouck Court, laid out in 1926, is located near the site of the former Gravesend Ship Canal. Bouck Street in the Bronx also honors him.

Bowery Street Named after the Bowery in Manhattan, this alley was once paved with planks to allow customers to make their way to Steeplechase founder George Tilyou's theater. It had been called Ocean View Walk, but its similarity to the Bowery in Manhattan with its theatrical lights and rowdy exuberance impelled the name change.

Bowery Street, 1903

Boynton Place Inventor (Eben) Moody Boynton (1840–1927) helped transpose bicycle technology to railroads. He expected his monorail "bicycle" trains to revolutionize railroading because they tripled a train's speed to an unheard of sixty miles per hour. The Boynton trains were test-run through Gravesend on the way to Brighton Beach, though they could never get enough financial backing to pass the demonstration point. For thirty years

Boynton appeared annually at New York's state house to pitch his invention. In 1920 his irrational entreaties to the Interstate Commerce Commission contributed to his undergoing "lunacy proceedings" in Washington (a jury acquitted him).

Bragg Street (see Batchelder Street)

Brigham Street (see Batchelder Street)

Calvert Vaux Park (Gravesend Bay, Bay 44th Street, Bay 49th Street, and Shore Parkway) It is fitting that the great London-born landscape architect of the nineteenth century and, with Frederick Law Olmsted, the person recognized for revolutionizing the concept and design of the public park would someday get a park named after him. Teamed with Olmsted, Calvert Vaux (1824–1895) was responsible for Brooklyn's Prospect Park and Fort Greene Park and for the laying out of Ocean and Eastern parkways. While visiting his son Bowyer in Bensonhurst, Vaux drowned in Gravesend Bay after falling off a pier in circumstances not fully understood. The *Brooklyn Daily Eagle* speculated that it was a suicide, but Vaux's family said he was without his glasses on a foggy day. The park is located near the spot of Vaux's demise.

Colby Court President Wilson's third secretary of state and later law partner, Bainbridge Colby (1869–1950) wrote the famous 1920 diplomatic note refusing to recognize the Soviet Union and calling the new country an enemy state. He had earlier joined forces with Teddy Roosevelt in the Bull Moose Party. A critic of FDR, Colby formed the American Liberty League in opposition to the New Deal, calling New Dealers "betrayers of the country." As a younger man, Colby was in the New York state assembly and as a lawyer once had the privilege of representing Mark Twain.

Colin Place The name likely refers to the great race horse Colin, known as the "Coney Island Horse," an undefeated thoroughbred that won the Belmont Stakes in 1908.

Contello Towers (Shore Parkway and Bay 43rd and 44th streets) A four-tower Bath Beach housing development overlooking the narrows, it is named for Anthony J. Contello, the city's first construction chief for its middle-income housing program.

Corbin Place Austin Corbin (1827–1896) was the developer of Manhattan Beach, a president of the Long Island Rail Road, and a notorious anti-Semite. After practicing law for many years, he moved to Coney Island in 1873 after his son took ill and the seaside resort appeared a good destination for recovery. While there, Corbin identified nearby Sedge Bank as an excellent real estate opportunity, purchased the property, and later renamed it Manhattan Beach. Exploiting his close relationship with John McKane, the corrupt head of the police force and unofficial "boss" of Coney Island, Corbin secured common lands for development. On Manhattan Beach he opened the luxurious Oriental and Manhattan Beach hotels. (At the latter, on opening day Ulysses S. Grant gave the dedication and John Philip Sousa first performed his "Stars and Stripes Forever.") Corbin was a member of the American Society for the Suppression of Jews and barred Jews from his premises. He once remarked, "If this is a free country, why can't we be free of the Jews?" and vowed to leave "nothing undone to get rid of them." He died in New Hampshire after a horse threw him from his carriage against a stone wall.

Coyle Street (see Batchelder Street)

Culver Plaza Currently the site of the New York Aquarium and once the home of Coney's famous Dreamland amusement park, it is named for attorney Andrew Culver, who in 1875 founded the Prospect Park and Coney Island Railroad. Culver also created the Coney Island Observatory and Signal Company and relocated an observatory tower (renamed the Iron Tower) from the Philadelphia Centennial Exposition (customers were charged fifteen cents to go up to the top on steam-run elevators). In 1893, Culver sold his railroad to Austin Corbin, the founder of Manhattan Beach. Today's F train is known as the Culver Line.

Dead Horse Bay The name says it all. An inlet located southwest of Floyd Bennett Field, this was the site from the 1850s to the 1930s where glue and other usable products were produced from the bones and carcasses of dead horses. It had been a part of Barren Island near Flatbush Avenue and populated by rugged villagers until Robert Moses cleared them for his Marine Parkway Bridge. In an inspiring twist of fate, the bay today has been reclaimed by its natural environment and is a choice site for winter duck spotting, nature trails, and fishing.

Dewey Albert Place (Corner of West 10th Street and Surf Avenue) Dewey Albert (1907–1992) and son Jerome were the cofounders of Astroland in 1962, today's resident amusement park in Coney Island. In 1975 the Alberts rehabilitated the venerated Cyclone roller coaster, now the park's most popular attraction. (It was designated a landmark in 1988.) Interestingly, Dewey Albert never intended to open an amusement park. He purchased the site on behalf of his friend Nathan Handwerker (see Nathan's Famous entry in this chapter), who planned to relocate his business to the spot. Nathan's never moved, and Albert began developing the amusement park Wonderland in the mid-1950s. The short street was named for the Alberts in 1997.

Dreier-Offerman Park (Bay 43–44th streets, Shore Parkway) The park was a gift of the Dreier family, who founded the charitable social-welfare organization for unwed mothers—the German Home for the Recreation of Women and Children—on this site. Iron merchant Theodor Dreier and his wife/cousin Dorothea Aldelheid Dreier led a prominent Brooklyn family immersed in the arts and progressive concerns. Their daughters shared considerable talent and commitment: Mary Dreier was active in suffrage issues and labor reform and became a friend to Eleanor Roosevelt; Margaret Dreier was the president of the New York branch of the Women's Trade Union League; and painter Katherine Sophie Dreier (1877–1952), who exhibited her work at the famous 1913 Armory show in New York, worked alongside the children of Theodor Offerman at the German Home. With her friend Marcel Duchamp she later helped establish the Société Anonyme —New York's first museum of modern art—to promote the efforts of the international avant-garde.

Emmons Avenue Patriarch of the family, Andries Emans, or Imans, came from England to Gravesend in 1661 on the ship *Saint Jean Baptist* by way of Leiden, Holland. He had many children including Jan Emans, who became Gravesend's deputy mayor, town clerk, and magistrate.

Fillmore Avenue/Fillmore Street America's thirteenth president, Millard Fillmore (1800–1874) of Buffalo, New York, came to power upon the midterm death of Whig president Zachary Taylor. In opposition to his boss, who wished to rid slavery from new states, Fillmore countered, "God knows that I detest slavery, but it is an existing evil . . . and we must endure it and give it such protection as is guaranteed by the Constitution." His signature on the Fugitive Slave Act sealed his fate with northern Whigs, who stymied his renomination in 1852. Fillmore later ran for president on the nativist Know-Nothing ticket and became a stern critic of Lincoln and Reconstruction, additional evidence of a flawed political career.

Millard Fillmore

Floyd Bennett Field Opened in 1931 as New York City's first municipal airport, Floyd Bennett Field is named for the aviator Floyd Bennett (1890–1928), whose 1926 flight over the North Pole with Commander Richard Byrd—the first such flight ever made—won him (and Byrd) a Congressional Medal of Honor.

Built on Barren Island, Floyd Bennett Field was a commercial failure, as it was always faster for Manhattan travelers to get to Newark Airport in New Jersey than to southern Brooklyn. Nonetheless, the airstrip held an appeal for pioneering aviators. During the 1930s "golden age of aviation" Amelia Earhart, Howard Hughes, and Wiley Post relied on Floyd Bennett Field for their record-breaking and publicity-generating flights. By 1941, however, Floyd Bennett Field had become a U.S. Naval Air Station, terminating all commercial travel. Today it is part of the National Park Service.

Ford Street (see Batchelder Street)

Gilmore Court Speculated to be named for Patrick Gilmore (1829–1892), the popular bandleader whose brass outfit was a fixture on Manhattan Beach starting in the late 1870s. Though born in Dublin, Gilmore became, according to the *Brooklyn Daily Eagle*, a "Brooklyn institution." Besides leading a band, Gilmore was also a songwriter who penned "When Johnny Comes Marching Home" under the pseudonym Louis Lambert. (Gilmore's band had served with a Union regiment during the Civil War.) John Philip Sousa replaced Gilmore as music director at the Manhattan Beach Hotel.

Guider Avenue Brooklyn Borough President Joseph Guider (1870–1926), whom Mayor Jimmy Walker eulogized as a "conscientious and useful public servant," also served as a Democratic assemblyman and Public Works commissioner. His commitment to improving Brooklyn included allowing bicyclists to cross the Brooklyn Bridge free of charge, widening streets and boulevards to reduce congestion, and helping establish what would become Brooklyn College. His labors to make Brooklyn more livable did not go unreciprocated: Guider Avenue today boasts Guider Mall, a handsome tree-lined pedestrian walkway.

Joseph Guider, mid-1920s

Gunnison Court Herbert F. Gunnison (1858–1932) was associated with Brooklyn's flagship publication, the *Brooklyn Daily Eagle*, from 1883 to 1929, until its sale to Frank Gannett. As publisher of the supplementary *Eagle Almanac*, Gunnison had the foresight to print William Tooker's writings on Long Island Indian place-names, later to become the standard work in the field. Gunnison was also the author of three books: *Out on Long Island*, *Flatbush of Today*, and *Two Americans in a Motor Car*.

Haring Street Named for the developer who from 1919 to 1922 purchased and developed the plots of land that make up Haring Street and Haring Playground. The area had been Sheepshead Bay Speedway, owned by the Whitney family; it was sold to a real estate company to pay off William C. Whitney's son's gambling debts (see Whitney Avenue entry in this chapter).

Hendrick I. Lott Homestead (1940 East 36th Street) Located in what was the southernmost point of the town of Flatlands, this landmarked 1800 Dutch colonial home went through eight generations from Hendrick I. Lott (1760–1840) to Ella Suydam (1897–1989). Curiously, the homestead is believed not only to have housed slaves—the Lotts were among the largest slaveholders in Brooklyn—but also to have later been a stop on the Underground Railroad.

Hendrick I. Lott House, 1923

Hendrickson Street In the mid- to late nineteenth century, John Hendrickson ran a general store and post office for the town of Flatlands that was located at the northeast corner of Flatbush and Kings Highway.

Hubbard Street The Hubbard family were landholders in Flatlands from 1652. Descendent and Revolutionary War patriot Elias Hubbard was one of Flatlands' leading funders of the colonists' cause. A 1790 census identifies his seventy-seven-acre farm and five slaves. In 1896 the farm was finally sold off. Hubbard Place, a segment of the former Hubbard Lane, survives south of Avenue K and Kings Highway.

Hunter Avenue Democratic mayor of Brooklyn John W(ard) Hunter (1807–1900) grew up in Bedford village and spent three decades as a New York customs house auditor. After the Civil War he served briefly in the U.S. Congress, where, allied with his fellow Democratic representatives, he helped obstruct Republican attempts to push ahead with Reconstruction. Within months of winning his seat, Hunter was censured for "unparliamentary language" and decided not to run again. After a period as a banker, Hunter was elected mayor of Brooklyn in 1873. Choosing to play hardball with fellow Brooklyn Tammany strongmen like Hugh McLaughlin—"such was his independence as mayor that his relations with the politicians were anything but pleasant," the *New York Times* wrote—Hunter would only see one term.

John Dewey High School (50 Avenue X) American philosopher, educator, and psychologist John Dewey (1859–1952) was a pioneer in progressive educational reform and a founder of one of the few uniquely American contributions to contemporary philosophy: pragmatism.

Knapp Street (see Batchelder Street)

Kouwenhoven Lane The Van Kouwenhoven (Cowenhoven) family, headed by patriarch Wolphert Gerritsen Van Kouwenhoven (1579–1662), emigrated from the Netherlands to New Utrecht in the seventeenth century and became prosperous landowners. Descendent Nicholas Cowenhoven (d. 1793) was a deserter from the patriot cause during the American Revolution and was indicted for treason. He had a remarkable turnaround, however, and ultimately became chief judge of the Court of Common Pleas of Kings County. The family name, which has taken on a multitude of spellings over the years, is remembered by a small lane that is a remnant of a much longer street.

Lady Moody Triangle (Village Road North, Lake Street, Avenue U) Early feminist, urban planner, and religious freedom activist Lady Deborah Moody (ca. 1583–1659) is a unique figure in Brooklyn's history. Born Deborah Dunch to a progressive English liberty-seeking family, Moody got caught up in the period's ongoing religious ferment. When England became uninviting for a person with her dissenting views, Moody sailed to the Massachusetts Bay Colony hoping for greater tolerance. Instead, still persecuted for her Anabaptism, she moved to what would become Gravesend. The first woman in the new world to receive (in 1645) an actual land patent, Moody is also considered one of the earliest town planners, laying out and dividing the area into four equally demarcated squares (the functional plan exists to this day). Because of her efforts, Gravesend became a haven for religious "nonconformists," most notably victimized Quakers harassed unrelentingly during Peter Stuyvesant's governorship.

Lama Court Representing a Brownsville district for thirty years, Democratic Brooklyn assemblyman Alfred Lama (1899–1984) is the namesake of this small lane as well as (one-half of) the well-known middle-income Mitchell-Lama housing law. Interestingly, the street's name predates Lama's political career; as a practicing architect he helped a local builder, who named the street in tribute to him.

Marine Park Brooklyn's largest park at 798 acres, it takes its name from the surrounding neighborhood. The two initial benefactors of Marine Park were Frederick B. Pratt and Alfred T. White, who gifted the city 150 acres for the park's construction in 1917 (an athletic field in the park now carries their names).

Marine Parkway – Gil Hodges Memorial Bridge Popular Brooklyn (and later Los Angeles) Dodger first baseman Gilbert Ray Hodges (1924–1972) slugged 370 home runs, and as manager of the once hapless New York Mets orchestrated their stunning 1969 World Series upset over the Baltimore Orioles. A well-worn anecdote describes how a Brooklyn priest during a 1953 heatwave and Hodges slump once told his parishioners, "It's too hot for a sermon. Keep the commandments and say a prayer for Gil Hodges." Hodges went on to bat .364 in the World Series that year. He died in 1972 after a massive heart attack following twenty-seven holes of golf. Opened in 1937 as the Marine Parkway Bridge, it was conamed in his honor in 1978.

Marine Parkway–Gil Hodges
Memorial Bridge

Marlboro Houses (between Stillwell Ave, 86th Street, Avenues X and Y) Named after the early-twentieth-century Marlboro section of Gravesend (now obsolete), the Marlboro Houses were completed in 1958 and comprise twenty-eight buildings. Of English origin, a more exalted spelling can be found with Marlborough Road in Flatbush (see chapter 5).

Mermaid Avenue Like neighboring Neptune Avenue, Mermaid Avenue suggests the fantastical, otherworldly seaside excitement of Coney Island. Commencing in 1983, the annual Mermaid Parade, a modern version of Coney Island's Mardi Gras (which ran from 1903 to 1954), finds participants dressing up as mermaids and other real and fictitious sea creatures. Folk icon Woody Guthrie spent his postwar years on the street, and *Mermaid Avenue,* the title of an album of Guthrie songs, was released posthumously.

Meucci Square (Avenue U, 86th Street, West 12th Street) It took over a century for Antonio Meucci (1808–1889), the rightful inventor of the telephone, to receive his proper due. Raised in Florence, Meucci made his initial discovery in Havana while working on electric-shock treatments for the ill. He had developed a working model already in 1859, seventeen years before Alexander Graham Bell's patent. After relocating to Staten Island, where he honed his prized invention (and intermittently housed the revolutionary Garibaldi), life proved tragic: he could not afford to patent his invention; was unable to get a meeting with the executives at Western Union to exhibit his genius; and was bested by Bell, his former lab-mate, who successfully secured a patent. There is a happy ending: the U.S. Congress in 2002 formally declared that Bell's patent was based on "fraud and misrepresentation" and recognized Meucci as the genuine inventor. The square was named in 1989, the centenary of Meucci's death.

Milton Berger Place (Surf Avenue between West 8th and West 10th streets) Brooklyn-born Milton Berger (1915–1997) was Coney Island's most famous press agent, with a client list that included Steeplechase Park, Astroland, and the Coney Island Chamber of Commerce. Called a "local landmark" by the *New York Times,* Berger was a relentless promoter of the island, whose "official" crowd estimates exaggerated the numbers to boost its popularity. Berger took a special interest in the Cyclone roller coaster and helped obtain its landmark status.

Nathan's Famous (corner of Stillwell and Surf avenues) Polish émigré and frankfurter entrepreneur Nathan Handwerker (1892–1974) is credited with popularizing the hot dog and making it a culinary staple for the working classes at Coney Island. He cut his teeth at the employ of Charles Feltman, the putative inventor of the frank in a bun, whose ten-cent hot dogs were all the rage at Coney Island in the early 1900s. Breaking out on his own in 1916, Handwerker halved the price to a nickel, and his business promptly skyrocketed. Advertising has always been the eatery's badge of pride, one historian writing that Nathan's signage "shriek[s] like fire-engine sirens."

Nellie Bly Park (1824 Shore Parkway at Twenty-sixth Avenue)

This amusement park, opened in 1966, is named for the celebrated muckraking investigative journalist who championed the rights of women and the disenfranchised. Born Elizabeth Jane Cochran (1867–1922) in Pennsylvania, she chose the pen name Nellie Bly (from the Stephen Foster song) upon launching her journalism career with the *Pittsburgh Dispatch*. Writing about the city's chronic social problems, Bly posed as a sweatshop worker to expose the wretched working conditions in Pittsburgh factories. Unable to continue when corporations threatened to cut their ad space, she traveled to Mexico to shed light on that country's poverty and corruption. Writing later for Joseph Pulitzer's *New York World*, Bly had herself committed to the Women's Lunatic Asylum at Blackwell Island (now Roosevelt Island) to report on the mistreatment of the mentally ill. This latter project provided the material for Bly's 1888 book *Ten Days in a Mad House*, and her exposé led to the asylum's eventual closing. Her record-breaking

Nellie Bly,
later nineteenth century

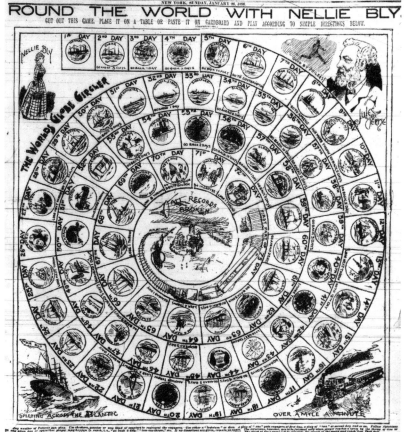

"Round the World with Nellie Bly—The Worlds Globe Circler," 1890

trip around the world in seventy-two days by train and steamer—she aspired to best the time set in Jules Verne's novel *Around the World in Eighty Days*—further cemented her celebrity status. Bly's spirit of adventure is the reason behind the amusement park's naming. When working in New York, she was a Brooklyn resident living on Marlborough Road in Flatbush.

Neptune Avenue (see Mermaid Avenue)

Nixon Court Naval architect, ship designer, and Tammany leader Lewis Nixon (1861–1940) was New York commissioner to the 1904 St. Louis World's Fair and president of the East River Bridge Commission (later the Williamsburg Bridge). After Secretary of the Navy William Whitney (see entry in this chapter) dispatched Nixon to view the great shipbuilding yards of Europe, Nixon was recruited by Tsar Nicholas II to design several ships for Russia. Closer to home, Nixon was a member of the Coney Island Jockey Club.

Oriental Boulevard Before Coney Island became proletarianized as the "nickel empire," together with Manhattan Beach the area was an elite resort enclave with some of the swankiest hotels on the East Coast. The 480-room Oriental Hotel, which gives the boulevard its name, was the brainchild of Austin Corbin (see entry in this chapter). It was in existence from 1880, when it was dedicated by President Rutherford B. Hayes, until 1916, and formed a pair with Corbin's magnificent Manhattan Beach Hotel (razed in 1907). The Oriental Hotel was the venue where Thomas Edison and Henry Ford first met during an 1896 electrical engineers convention.

Oriental Hotel, 1904

Pieter Claesen Wyckoff House (5816 Clarendon Road) Occupied by Wyckoff descendents until 1902, the Flatlands Dutch-colonial farmhouse is the oldest (ca. 1652) house in New York City and one of the oldest frame houses in the United States. Pieter Claesen Wyckoff (see chapter 3) acquired the land by means of his association with Peter Stuyvesant. In 1965, it was the first structure landmarked in New York City.

Pieter Claesen Wyckoff House, 1922

Plumb Beach Once called Plumb Island, it is named for the fruit formerly abundant in the vicinity.

Quentin Road Formerly Avenue Q, it was renamed after World War I for Quentin Roosevelt (1897–1918), the youngest (and favorite) son of the twenty-sixth president. Like Sgt. Joyce Kilmer (see entry in this chapter), Roosevelt was killed in France on active duty during World War I.

Riegelmann Boardwalk Now one of the area's most recognizable features, the Boardwalk opened in 1923, over a decade after it was first proposed. Its establishment was encouraged by Edward A. Riegelmann (1869–1941), supreme court justice, head of the New York City Street Opening Bureau, and Brooklyn borough president at the time of the Boardwalk's construction. Nicknamed "Coney Island's Fifth Avenue," it was likened by French

Riegelmann Boardwalk, 1983

prime minister Edouard Herriot to the "Promenade des Anglais at Nice turned over to the proletariat."

Royce Street Named after the mother of Charles Ward, the commissioner of Borough Works.

Schweickerts Walk Early-twentieth-century Coney Island businessman Philip Schweickert worked with other German congregants of St. Paul's Lutheran Church to promote the interests of the amusement industry and protect what they saw as their constitutionally guaranteed right to property. With other wealthy residents, Schweickert founded the Coney Island Taxpayers Alliance, an organization that fought civic groups seeking to open a public beach (the Alliance lost). The street name is bereft of an apostrophe.

Sea Gate Originally called Coney Island Point, the island's western tip once boasted the first amusement in the area, Alonzo Reed's 1840s Pavillion dance hall. Three decades later the name was changed to Norton's Point, after Tammany Hall politician Michael "Thunderbolt" Norton. Notorious for its underworld activity and lawless behavior, Norton's Point is where Boss Tweed sought refuge upon escaping from jail and before sailing to Spain. At the century's end it was sold again, this time to the Norton Point Land Company, and renamed the anodyne Sea Gate for its geographic placement as gatekeeper to the water. A private gated beachfront community, it became home to Al Smith and Beverly Sills.

Stillwell Avenue Early settler Nicholas Stillwell (1603–1671), progenitor of the prominent Stillwell family of Gravesend, arrived in Virginia with his family in 1638. (Devout Calvinists, they had earlier left England for the Netherlands.) Removing later to New Amsterdam, Stillwell became the owner of a large farm, where he settled with his wife and eleven children. He sided with the Dutch against the English takeover in 1664, and a century later his residence was used as a government storehouse during the Revolutionary War. Descendent William Stillwell, Gravesend town surveyor in the 1860s, abused his official position and pocketed money from developers William Engemen and Austin Corbin (see entry in this chapter) for assisting them in securing sweetheart deals for the eastern half of Coney Island.

Stillwell Avenue is memorable to film buffs because of the *French Connection*'s chase scene, which took place under and on the West End Line (it was the B train, now the D line).

Stratton-Henderson Walk Anson Stratton, a friend of Coney Island political boss John McKane, developed a number of dance halls along Coney Island's Bowery. Impresario Fred Henderson built a vaudeville theater in Coney Island, followed later by a music hall and restaurant. When an 1899 fire on the Bowery burned down his and other establishments, the local building commissioner called it an act of "divine providence." Together, Stratton and Henderson opened a bathhouse in 1895.

Stryker Court/Stryker Street Burdett Stryker held several occupations including butcher, ferryman, and tallow chandler and from 1839 to 1849 served as chief engineer of the volunteer fire department. His son, prominent Whig politician and Brooklyn mayor Francis Burdett Stryker (1811–1892), is better remembered in the annals of Brooklyn history; he was reelected twice in 1847 and 1848 (mayors then were elected annually) and is recognized for his efforts to protect residents from cholera and other diseases.

Van Sicklen Street (see Van Siclen Avenue, chapter 6)

Voorhies Avenue Original descendent Steven Coerte Van Voorhees (1600–1677) arrived in Flatlands in 1660 (the surname means "from" [*Van*] "before" [*Voor*] "the village of Hees"; the "Van" was later dropped). Voorhees was a magistrate and an elder at the local Dutch Reformed church.

Whitney Avenue Wealthy New York financier William Collins Whitney (1841–1904) was a fierce opponent of Tammany Hall who contributed to Boss Tweed's downfall and reform governor Samuel Tilden's ascent (see chapter 5). Whitney later served as secretary of the navy in Grover Cleveland's first administration. (Though affiliated with the Democratic Party he was called a "Republican by nature and a Democrat by association.") Whitney's interest in horse racing was great later in life, and his Sheepshead Bay estate (one of many) of three hundred acres was situated near the Belmont and Gravesend racetracks. Whitney's daughter, Dorothy Whitney, helped found the *New Republic* magazine and the New School for Social Research.

Illustration Sources

Works Consulted

Abel, Allen. *Flatbush Odyssey: A Journey through the Heart of Brooklyn.* Toronto, Canada: McClelland and Stewart, 1995.

Allbray, Nedda C. *Flatbush: The Heart of Brooklyn.* Charleston, SC: Arcadia, 2004.

Armbruster, Eugene. *Brooklyn's Eastern District.* New York: n.p., 1912.

———. *Coney Island.* New York: n.p., 1924.

Ashley, Leonard R. N. *What's in a Name? Everything You Wanted to Know.* Baltimore, MD: Genealogical Publishing Company, 1989.

Bennett, Gertrude Ryder. *Living in a Landmark.* Francestown, NH: Marshall Jones Company, 1980.

———. *Turning Back the Clock in Gravesend: Background of the Wyckoff-Bennett Homestead.* Francestown, NH: Marshall Jones, 1982.

Benzaia, Diana. "Place Names in Selected Areas of Brooklyn: The Heart of New Utrecht." Master's thesis, Brooklyn College, 1970.

Berman, John S. *Coney Island.* New York: Museum of the City of New York (Portraits of America), 2003.

Brown, Joshua, and David Ment. *Factories, Foundries, and Refineries: A History of Five Brooklyn Industries.* Brooklyn, NY: Brooklyn Rediscovery; Brooklyn Educational and Cultural Alliance, 1980.

Buckman, Gertrude. "Place-Names in Greenpoint." Master's thesis, Brooklyn College, 1966.

Burrows, Edwin G., and Mike Wallace. *Gotham: A History of New York City to 1898.* New York: Oxford University Press, 2000.

Cannato, Vincent. *The Ungovernable City: John Lindsay and His Struggle to Save New York.* New York: Basic Books, 2001.

Christman, Henry M., ed. *Walt Whitman's New York: From Manhattan to Montauk.* New York: New Amsterdam Books, 1963.

Conklin, William J., and Jeffrey Simpson. *Brooklyn's City Hall.* New York: City of New York, Department of General Services, 1983.

Connally, Harold X. *A Ghetto Grows in Brooklyn.* New York: New York University Press, 1977.

Cudahy, Brian. *The Malbone Street Wreck.* New York: Fordham University Press, 2000.

Custer, E. A. *A Synoptical History of the Towns of Kings County from 1525 to Modern Times: Containing the Origin of the Names of the Streets, Avenues, and Lanes. / Compiled [by E. A. Custer] from the Manuscripts of Stiles, Ostrander, Furnam, and Other Historians.* New York: Sherwood, 1886.

Denson, Charles. *Coney Island: Lost and Found.* Berkeley, CA: Ten Speed Press, 2002.

Dolkart, Andrew S., and Tony Velez. *This Is Brooklyn: A Guide to the Borough's Historic Districts and Landmarks.* Brooklyn, NY: Fund for the Borough of Brooklyn, 1990.

Federal Writers' Project of the Works Progress Administration in New York City. *The*

WPA Guide to New York City: The Federal Writers' Project Guide to 1930s New York: A Comprehensive Guide to the Five Boroughs of the Metropolis — Manhattan, Brooklyn, the Bronx, Queens, and Richmond. New York: New Press, 1992.

Feirstein, Sanna. *Naming New York: Manhattan Places and How They Got Their Names.* New York: New York University Press, 2001.

Fischler, Stan. *Confessions of a Trolley Dodger from Brooklyn.* Flushing, NY: H&M Productions II, 1995.

Freudenheim, Ellen. *Brooklyn! A Soup-to-Nuts Guide to Sights, Neighborhoods, and Restaurants.* New York: St. Martin's Griffin, 1999.

Freudenheim, Ellen, with Daniel P. Wiener. *Brooklyn: Where to Go, What to Do, How to Get There.* New York: St. Martin's Press, 1991.

Fund for the Borough of Brooklyn. *Brooklyn Neighborhood Book.* Brooklyn, NY: Fund for the Borough of Brooklyn, 1985.

Glueck, Grace, and Paul Gardner. *Brooklyn: People and Places, Past and Present.* New York: Abrams, 1991.

Graves, Horace. *History in the Streets; or, Some of the Historical Associations of the Streets of Brooklyn.* Brooklyn, NY: n.p., 1894.

Guthman, Joel I. *Brooklyn Street Names: In the Area Bounded by Myrtle Avenue, Broadway, Fulton Street and Franklin Avenue.* Brooklyn, NY: s.n., 1967.

———. *Brooklyn Streets Named for the Signers of the Declaration of Independence.* Brooklyn, NY: Office of the President, Borough Brooklyn, 1966.

Habenstrat, Barbara. *Fort Greene, U.S.A.* New York: Bobbs-Merrill, 1974.

Haber, Richard. "Gravesend Place Names." Master's thesis, Brooklyn College, 1964.

Hoffman, Jerome F. X. *The Bay Ridge Chronicles: 1524–1976.* Brooklyn, NY: Bay Ridge Bicentennial Committee of the Planning Board 10, 1976.

Ierardi, Eric J. *Images of America: Brooklyn in the 1920s.* Charleston, SC: Arcadia, 1998.

———. *Images of America: Gravesend, Brooklyn: Coney Island and Sheepshead Bay.* Dover, NH: Arcadia, 1996.

Immerso, Michael. *Coney Island: The People's Playground.* New Brunswick, NJ: Rutgers University Press, 2002.

Jackson, Kenneth, ed. *The Encyclopedia of New York City.* New Haven, CT: Yale University Press, 1995.

———. *The Neighborhoods of Brooklyn.* New Haven, CT: Yale University Press/Citizens Committee for New York City, 1998.

Kamil, Seth, and Eric Wakin. *The Big Onion Guide to Brooklyn: Ten Historic Walking Tours.* New York: New York University Press, 2005.

Kasson, John. *Amusing the Millions.* New York: Hill and Wang, 1978.

Kazin, Alfred. *A Walker in the City.* New York: Harcourt, Brace, 1951.

Kramer, Ruth. "Place Names in Bushwick." Master's thesis, Brooklyn College, 1971.

Kroessler, Jeffrey A. *New York, Year by Year: A Chronology of the Great Metropolis.* New York: New York University Press, 2002.

Lancaster, Clay. *Old Brooklyn Heights: New York's First Suburb including Detailed Analysis of 61 Century-Old Houses.* Rutland, VT: Charles E. Tuttle, 1961.

———. *Prospect Park Handbook.* New York: Published for Greensward Foundation by Long Island University Press, 1972.

Landesman, Alter F. *Brownsville: The Birth, Development, and Passing of a Jewish Community in New York*. New York: Bloch, 1969.

Landmarks Preservation Commission. *Greenpoint Historic District Designation Report, City of New York*. New York: Landmarks Preservation Commission, 1982.

Latimer, Margaret. *Two Cities: New York and Brooklyn the Year the Great Bridge Opened*. Brooklyn, NY: Brooklyn Educational and Cultural Alliance, 1983.

————, ed. *Brooklyn Almanac: Illustrations, Facts, Figures, People, Buildings, Books*. Brooklyn, NY: Brooklyn Rediscovery; Brooklyn Educational and Cultural Alliance, 1984.

Linder, Marc, and Lawrence S. Zacharias. *Of Cabbages and Kings County*. Iowa City: University of Iowa Press, 1999.

Lockwood, Charles. *Bricks and Brownstone: The New York Row House, 1783–1929*. New York: Rizzoli, 2003.

Lopate, Carol. *Education and Culture in Brooklyn: A History of Ten Institutions*. Brooklyn, NY: Brooklyn Educational and Cultural Alliance, 1979.

Marlow, Nicholas J. "Bedford-Stuyvesant Place-Names." Master's thesis, Brooklyn College, 1963.

McCullough, David W. *Brooklyn, and How It Got That Way*. New York: Dial Press, 1983.

————. *Great Bridge: The Epic Story of the Building of the Brooklyn Bridge*. Simon and Schuster, 1983.

McNamara, John. *History in Asphalt: The Origin of Bronx Street and Place Names*. Bronx, NY: Bronx Historical Society, 1991.

Ment, David. *The Shaping of a City: A Brief History of Brooklyn*. Brooklyn, NY: Brooklyn Rediscovery; Brooklyn Educational and Cultural Alliance, 1979.

Ment, David, and Mary Donovan. *The People of Brooklyn: A History of Two Neighborhoods*. Brooklyn, NY: Brooklyn Educational and Cultural Alliance, 1980.

Ment, David, with Anthony Robins and David Framberger. *Building Blocks of Brooklyn: A Study of Urban Growth*. Brooklyn, NY: Brooklyn Rediscovery: Brooklyn Educational and Cultural Alliance, 1979.

Merlis, Brian. *Brooklyn — The Centennial Edition: Celebrating the Borough's 100th Anniversary*. Brooklyn, NY: Israelowitz Press, 1998.

————. *Brooklyn-The Way It Was*. Brooklyn, NY: Israelowitz Press, 1995.

Merlis, Brian, and Lee A. Rosenzweig. *Brooklyn Heights and Downtown: Volume 1, 1860–1922*. Brooklyn, NY: Israelowitz Publishing in association with Brooklyn Editions, 2001.

————. *Brooklyn's Park Slope: A Photographic Retrospective*. New York: Sheepshead Bay Historical Society and Israelowitz Press, 1999.

Merlis, Brian, Lee A. Rosenzweig, and I. Stephen Miller. *Brooklyn's Gold Coast: The Sheepshead Bay Communities*. New York: Sheepshead Historical Society with Israelowitz Press and Brooklyn Editions, 1997.

Miller, Ruth Seiden, ed. *Brooklyn U.S.A.* Brooklyn, NY: Brooklyn College Press, 1979.

Minsky, Pearl. "Canarsie Place Names." Masters thesis, Brooklyn College, 1963.

Morrone, Francis, and James Iska. *An Architectural Guidebook to Brooklyn*. Layton, UT: Gibbs Smith, 2001.

Moscow, Henry. *The Street Book: An Encyclopedia of Manhattan's Street Names and Their Origins.* New York: Fordham University Press, 1990.

Nelson, Derek. *Off the Map: The Curious Histories of Place-Names.* New York: Kodansha International, 1997.

New York City Landmarks Commission, Andrew Dolkart, ed. *Guide to New York City Landmarks.* Washington, DC: Preservation Press, 1992.

Pearlman, Archie. "East New York Place Names." Master's thesis, Brooklyn College, 1965.

Rashkin, Henry. "Bay Ridge Place Names." Master's thesis, Brooklyn College, 1960.

Reiss, Marcia. *Neighborhood History Guide: Red Hook and Gowanus.* Brooklyn, NY: Brooklyn Historical Society, 2000.

———. *Neighborhood History Guide: Williamsburg.* Brooklyn, NY: Brooklyn Historical Society, 2000.

Richman, Jeffrey I. *Brooklyn's Green-Wood Cemetery: New York's Buried Treasure.* Lunenburg, VT: Stinehour Press, 1998.

Richmond, John, and Abril Lamarque. *Brooklyn, U.S.A.* New York: Creative Age Press, 1946.

Rieder, Jonathan. *Canarsie: The Jews and Italians of Brooklyn against Liberalism.* Cambridge, MA: Harvard University Press, 1985.

Rubel, Tamara. "Place Names in Brooklyn Heights." Master's thesis, Brooklyn College, 1963.

Sanchez, Toby. *The Bedford Stuyvesant Neighborhood Profile.* Brooklyn, NY: Brooklyn in Touch Information Center, 1993.

Scarpa, Peter, Lawrence Stelter, and Peter Syrdal. *Bay Ridge.* Charleston, SC: Bay Ridge Historical Society; Arcadia, 2001.

Schecter, Irwin. "Place-Names in Olympia." Master's thesis, Brooklyn College, 1970.

Schroth, Raymond A. *The Eagle and Brooklyn: A Community Newspaper, 1841–1955.* Westport, CT: Greenwood Press, 1954.

Sherman, Herman. "Red Hook Place-Names." Master's thesis, Brooklyn College, 1965.

Snyder, John J. *Tales of Old Flatbush.* Brooklyn, NY: City of New York, 1945.

Snyder-Grenier, Ellen M. *Brooklyn! An Illustrated History.* Philadelphia: Temple University Press, 1996.

Stayton, Kevin L. *Dutch by Design: Tradition and Change in Two Historic Brooklyn Houses: The Schenk Houses at the Brooklyn Museum.* New York: Brooklyn Museum/Phaidon Universe, 1990.

Stewart, George R. *American Place-Names: A Concise and Selective Dictionary for the Continental United States of America.* New York: Oxford University Press, 1970.

Stiles, Henry Reed. *A History of the City of Brooklyn: Including the Old Town and Village of Brooklyn, the Town of Bushwick, and the Village and City of Williamsburg.* Brooklyn, NY: Published by subscription, 1867–1870.

Stonehill, Judith, and Francis Morrone. *Brooklyn: A Journey through the City of Dreams.* New York: Universe, 2004.

Sullivan, Neil J. *The Dodgers Move West.* New York: Oxford University Press, 1987.

Tooker, William Wallace. *Indian Names of Places in the Borough of Brooklyn: With Historical and Ethnological Notes.* New York: F. P. Harper, ca. 1901.

Trachtenberg, Alan. *Brooklyn Bridge: Fact and Symbol.* Chicago: University of Chicago Press, 1965.

Vasiliev, Ren. *From Abbotts to Zurich: New York State Placenames.* Syracuse, NY: Syracuse University Press, 2004.

Weld, Ralph Foster. *Brooklyn Is America.* New York: Columbia University Press, 1950.

———. *Our Brooklyn.* Brooklyn, NY: Brooklyn Institute of Arts and Sciences, 1940.

Wells, Cornelius L. *Quarter Millennial Anniversary of the Reformed Dutch Church of Flatbush, New York.* n.p., 1904.

Weyant, Morrison V. R. *The Romance in the History of Street Names in Brooklyn: The Story of Keap Street, Brooklyn Eastern District of the 1830s.* Brooklyn, NY: Burwey Press, 1928.

White, Norval, and Elliot Willensky. *AIA Guide to New York City,* 4th ed. New York: Crown, 2000.

Wilder, Craig Steven. *A Covenant with Color: Race and Social Power in Brooklyn 1636–1990.* New York: Columbia University Press, 2000.

Willensky, Elliot. *When Brooklyn Was the World: 1920–1957.* New York: Harmony Books, 1986.

Wolfe, Gerard R. *New York: 15 Walking Tours: An Architectural Guide to the Metropolis.* New York: McGraw Hill, 2003.

Wright, Carol von Pressentin, Stuart Miller, and Sharon Seitz. *New York (Blue Guide).* London: A & C Black, 2002.

Index

Button, Dick, 74
Butts, Richard, 58
Byrd, Richard, 163
Byrne, James J., 66

Cadman, Samuel Parkes, 42
Cadman Plaza, 42
Calder, William Musgrave, 62, *62*
Calder Place, 62
Calhoun, John C., 15, 96
Calhoun Street, 15
Calvert Vaux Park, 161
Calyer, Jacobus, 15
Calyer Street, 15
Cambridge Place, 2, 81
Campbell, Patrick, 67
Campus Road, 104
Canarsee Indians, 3, 11, 57, 104, 109, 122, 139, 157, 158
Canarsie, 1, 122
Cannonball Park (John Paul Jones Park), 144, *144*
Capone, Al, 70
Carl, Willie, 126
Carleton, Lord (Henry Boyle), 81
Carlton Avenue, 81–82
Carlton Gardens, 82
Carlton House, 81–82
Carlton House Terrace, 82
Carroll, Charles, 58, *62*, 62–63
Carroll Gardens, 58
Carroll Street, 62–63
Carroll Street, Number 1150 (Medgar Evers College), 92
Carthan, Hattie, 91
Carty, John J., 143
Carver, George Washington, 82
Carver Playground, 82
Cashmore, John, 40
Cathedral Place, 42
Catherine Street Ferry, 61
Caton, Margaret, 105, 106
Caton, Susan Martense, 105
Caton Avenue, 105, *105*
Cedar Place. *See* McKeever Place
Cemetery of the Evergreens, 123
Central Congregational Church, 42
Chapel Street, 42
Chapin, Harry, 46
Charles II, King of England, 3
Charles Pratt Home, *93*

Chauncey, Isaac, 82, 96
Chauncey Street, 82
Cheever, Samuel, 63
Cheever Place, 63
Chisholm, Shirley, 107
Christ Church, 147, 148
Christ Church and Holy Family, 71
Church, William, 115
Church Avenue, 105
Church City Nines. *See* Brooklyn Dodgers
Church Lane. *See* Church Avenue
Church of the Assumption, 70
Church of the Generals. *See* St. John's Episcopal Church
Church of the Holy Trinity. *See* St. Ann and the Holy Trinity Church
Churchill, Randolph, 127
Churchill, Winston, 126
Circumferential Parkway. *See* Shore Parkway
City Hall. *See* Brooklyn Borough Hall
Claesen, Pieter (Pieter Wyckoff), 2, 72, 82, 116, 171
Clara Barton High School, 82
Clara Street, 105
Clarendon Road, Number 5816 (Pieter Claesen Wyckoff House), 171, *171*
Clark, William, 42
Clark Street, 42
Clarkson, Matthew, 105–106
Clarkson Avenue, 105–106
Classon Avenue, 82
Classon Avenue, Number 901 (Clara Barton High School), 82
Clay, Henry, 96
Clay, Humphrey, 15
Clay Street, 15
Clemente, Roberto, 27
Clermont Avenue, 82–83
Clermont (steamship), 45, 82–83
Cleveland, Grover, 124, 126, 132, 173
Cleveland Street, 124
Clift, Montgomery, 73
Clifton, Robert, 83
Clifton Place, 83
Clinton, DeWitt, 46, 61, 65, 76, 83
Clinton, George, 17, 60, 83, 107
Clinton, James, 83
Clinton Avenue, 83
Clinton Avenue, Number 77 (Benjamin Banneker Academy), 80

Van Brunt, Rutgert Joesten, 71
Van Brunt Street, 71
Van Buren, Martin, 96, 97
Van Buren Street, 97
Van Dam, Anthony, 30
Van Dam, Rip, 30
Van Dam Street, 29–30
Van Doren, Isaac, 42
Van Doren, Jacob L., 42
Van Dyck, Jan Thomasse, 72
Van Dyke, Matthias, 72
Van Dyke, Nicholas, 72
Van Dyke Street, 72
Van Nostrand, Hans Hansen, 92–93
Van Sicklen family, 121, 124, 127, 128, 132
Van Sicklen Street. *See* Van Siclen Avenue
Van Siclen Avenue, 132
Van Siclen farmhouse, *133*
Van Sinderen, Adriaen, 133
Van Sinderen, Hotse, 133
Van Sinderen, Ulpianus, 133
Van Sinderen Avenue, 133, *133*
Van Sinderen family, 121
Van Twiller, Wouter, 104
Vanderbeek, Rem Jansen, 50–51
Vanderbilt, Cornelius, 13
Vanderbilt, Gertrude Lefferts, 113
Vanderbilt, Jan Aertsen, 113
Vanderbilt, John, 104, 110, 113
Vanderbilt family, 104
Vanderbilt Street, 113
Vanderveer, Cornelis Janszen, 113–114
Vanderveer, Gerret, 114
Vanderveer, John C., 114
Vanderveer, Peter, 134
Vanderveer Estates, 114
Vanderveer family, 104, 121
Vanderveer Park, 114, 134
Vanderveer Place, 114
Varick, Richard, 30
Varick Avenue/Varick Street, 30
Varkens Hook Road, 133–134
Vaux, Bowyer, 161
Vaux, Calvert, 72, 84, 86, 111, 161
Vechte, Claes Arentson, 68
Vechte, Nicholas, 68–69
Vechte-Cortelyou House/Old Stone House, 63, 66, *66*, 68–69, 70
Vernon Avenue. *See* Tilden Avenue
Veronica Place, 115

Verrazano–Narrows Bridge, 4, 139, 145, 150, *151*
Verrazzano, Giovanni da, 150
Vienna Avenue. *See* Lorraine Avenue
Vincent Gardenia Boulevard, 150
Vinegar Hill, 37
Visitation of the Blessed Virgin Mary Church, 72
Visitation Place, 72
V'Lacke Bos, 2
Volckertsen, Dirck ("the Norman"), 20, 26
von Mises, Ludwig, 104
Voorhees, Coerte Van, 173
Voorhies Avenue, 173

W. Beard and Robinson Stores, 59
Wakeman, Abram, 150–151
Wakeman Place, 150–151
Walker, Jimmy, 114–115, 164
Wall Street. *See* Arion Place
Wallabout Bay, 4, 30, 37
Wallabout Street, 30
Wallace, Mike, 96
Wallaston Court, 151
Wallaston Realty Company, 151
Walt Whitman Houses, 97
Walton, George, 30
Walton Street, 30
Ward, Charles, 172
Washington, George, 30, 44, 47, 58, 62, 64, 71, 76, 80, 84, 86, 87, 90, 94, 107
Washington Avenue Baptist Church, 86
Washington Crossing the Delaware (painting), 31
Washington Hall Park, 97
Washington Park (Brooklyn Dodgers ballfield), 85
Washington Park (later Fort Greene Park), 86
Washington Park (street), 97
Waterbury, Noah, 30
Waterbury Street, 30
Watkins Street, Number 440 (Nehemiah Houses), 128
Webb, Eckford, 17
Webb & Bell, 17
Weeks, James, 77
Weeksville, 77, 84, 88–89
Weir, James, 139
Weirfield, Thomas, 30
Weirfield Street, 30
Weld, Ralph Foster, 1
Wells, John D., 123

About the Authors

Leonard Benardo is the author of several chapters in both the *Big Onion Guide to New York City* (NYU Press, 2002) and the *Big Onion Guide to Brooklyn* (NYU Press, 2005) and is a contributor to the *Encyclopedia of New York* (Syracuse University Press, 2005) and *The New Grove Dictionary of Jazz* (Macmillan, 2002). Jennifer Weiss is the coeditor of *Eldercare in New York* (FRIA, 1999) and has been published in the *Washington Post, New York Newsday,* and the *New York Law Journal.* Leonard and Jennifer live in Brooklyn with their son, Felix, and daughter, Anya.